PRAISE FOR
THE INTROVERT'S EDGE TO

"This is the networking blueprint that will change your life—a proven approach written by someone who's actually done it. If you're looking for an actionable guide to genuine and effective networking, this is it."
—Neil Patel, Cofounder of NP Digital, *Wall Street Journal* Top Influencer, *Forbes* Top 10 Marketer, and *New York Times* Bestselling Author

"I often say that the secret to winning is helping others win, a philosophy clearly shared by Pollard. For introverts who shudder at the idea of working a room, this refreshing guide is a long-awaited answer. Embrace this practical and proven method for creating powerful, authentic, and mutually beneficial connections."
—Marshall Goldsmith, Thinkers50 Hall of Fame Inductee, and *New York Times* Bestselling Author of *Triggers*, *MOJO*, and *What Got You Here Won't Get You There*

"As Matthew Pollard so adeptly explains, successful networking isn't about trying to be someone you're not but using your natural gifts to become who you were always meant to be. Sage advice for all entrepreneurs!"
—Michael E. Gerber, Creator of the *New York Times* mega-bestselling E-Myth books

"As an introvert myself, I founded BNI as a way to add structure to the uncomfortable process of networking. Matthew's guidance takes this concept of framework and standardization to the next level, offering a meaningful strategy that works in any room, for any introverted business professional."
—Dr. Ivan Misner, Founder of BNI and *New York Times* Bestselling Author

"Step by step, Pollard teaches introverts how to master networking and authentically build a community of mutually supportive contacts. A must-read for anyone looking for an achievable and practical framework for creating productive professional relationships."
—Mark Roberge, Senior Lecturer at Harvard Business School, Managing Director of Stage 2 Capital, and Former CRO of HubSpot

"Matthew Pollard provides a winning formula for creating powerful, authentic connections. He masterfully confronts the stigma around the so-called extroverted arena of networking, demonstrating that introverts have exactly what it takes to outshine everyone else in the room."

—Derek Lidow, Chair of the Entrepreneurship Faculty, Princeton University, and Author of *Startup Leadership* and *Building on Bedrock*

"Matthew Pollard is emerging as America's #1 introvert converter. Focusing on the value of networking as an introvert, he will give you ideas and strategies to beat the extroverts, every time."

—Jeffrey Gitomer, Author of the *Little Red Book of Selling*

"A smart, motivating, and practical system for getting influential connections excited about promoting you and your work. Using a combination of generosity, authenticity, strategy, and a heartfelt desire to help others, Matthew shows introverts how to turn networking from dreadful and pointless to profitable and valuable. Best of all, I have personally experienced how Matthew lives out the words in this book. I can say wholeheartedly that if you practice what this book teaches, you will grow and serve others like never before."

—Tom Ziglar, CEO of Ziglar, Inc.

"Matthew Pollard's entertaining and clever book on how introverts can network successfully has a hidden bonus. It also offers leaders guidance on how to create truly inclusive teams and cultures—where both extroverts and introverts thrive."

—Michael C. Bush, Global CEO of Great Place to Work®

"A must for any professional, *The Introvert's Edge to Networking* breaks through long-believed myths and explains exactly why introverts are perfectly suited to mastering the room. Matthew shows you how to develop relationships that will change your life!"

—Tom Dekle, Vice President of Digital Sales at IBM, AA-ISP Board Member, and Inside Sales Lifetime Achievement Recipient

"Imagine going into a networking room knowing exactly who you're going to speak to, exactly what you'll say, and exactly how you'll follow up. Imagine confidently building a network of supportive, mutually beneficial contacts who love your work and are willing to go to bat for you. Now read this book and make it happen."

—Verne Harnish, Founder of Entrepreneurs' Organization and Author of *Scaling Up*

"If you have an exceptional offering, yet no one 'gets it,' Pollard's book is for you."

—Mike Michalowicz,
Author of *Fix This Next* and *Profit First*

"As a digital marketer, I know how crucial it is to validate your message in the real world before taking it online. But as an introvert, I also know how unbearable it can be to actually work the room. Pollard's brilliant system gives you the best of both worlds—a foolproof way to network strategically while getting your message exactly right."

—Ryan Deiss, CEO of DigitalMarketer.com

"I always suggest that my students and small business clients focus on strategy in any business endeavor. When it comes to networking, though, there's a misconception that it's all about personality; strategy is a distant second, if it's mentioned at all. Pollard upends this paradigm, showing that win-win networking can be systemized and mastered by even the quietest introverts. This book will help you portray the best, most confident version of yourself in the most important component of personal and business success—effective networking."

—Greg Tucker, State Director of Small
Business Development Centers, Missouri

"As an introvert myself, I know that many of us struggle to comfortably and authentically develop connections. Pollard provides a clear-eyed, practical guide for introverts who want to network their way to new heights."

—Dorie Clark, Thinkers50 Top Business Thinker,
HBR Contributor and Bestselling Author

"Through multiple engaging stories, Matthew Pollard shares practical advice to help introverts use their strengths to build their personal and professional networks. If you find networking a dreadful, but necessary, chore, Matthew will provide you with useful strategies and language to make the process much more accessible."

—Nancy Ancowitz, Author of *Self-Promotion for Introverts*®

"The tactical, practical, and highly actionable advice Pollard provides introverts will not only arm them with science-backed processes and greater networking success but will, dare I say it, leave the extroverts shaking their heads, wondering how they can capture some of this magic."

—Anthony Iannarino, Author of *The Only Sales Guide
You'll Ever Need* and Cofounder of the OutBound Conference

"In this fresh and original book, Matthew challenges all our preconceptions about what makes a successful networker. Destined to be a classic in business and self-help literature."

—Judy Robinett, Author of *How to Be a Power Connector*
(listed as the best business book of 2014 by *Inc.*
and a must-read book by *Success* magazine)

"Being an introvert can be your superpower, especially if you use it to your advantage. Pollard shows you how to channel your networking efforts into actionable steps through a perfect combination of authenticity and ambition."

—Tiffani Bova, Global Growth Evangelist at Salesforce
and the *Wall Street Journal* Bestselling Author of *Growth IQ*

"In this highly readable and engaging book, Pollard shares how introverts can painlessly and enjoyably build valuable relationships and business connections. This networking system will change your professional life."

—Jake Tatel, one of the world's leading technology innovators

"As an introverted executive operating in a seemingly extroverted world, I struggle with many of the challenges that Pollard outlines in *The Introvert's Edge to Networking*. Using real-world examples and powerful evidence, this book has given me the tools to leverage authenticity and take a smarter approach to optimize my networking ability."

—Donald Thomas, Vice President and General
Manager of Bloomberg Government

"Introverts know that networking is crucial to career success, yet they are rightly reluctant to morph into extroverts to get it done. This engaging book draws from the author's own learnings and the struggles and triumphs of others to show us how introverts can use their natural strengths to become superb networkers."

—Jennifer B. Kahnweiler, PhD, CSP, and Bestselling Author of
Creating Introvert-Friendly Workplaces and *The Introverted Leader*

"Thanks to the strategies you'll discover in this book, my team dramatically increased donations without feeling uncomfortable. If you're looking for a way to help your team have the right conversations and raise the critical dollars needed to support your cause, this is it."

—Jennifer Stolo, Chapter President and CEO
of the Make-A-Wish Foundation

THE
introvert's
EDGE
TO NETWORKING

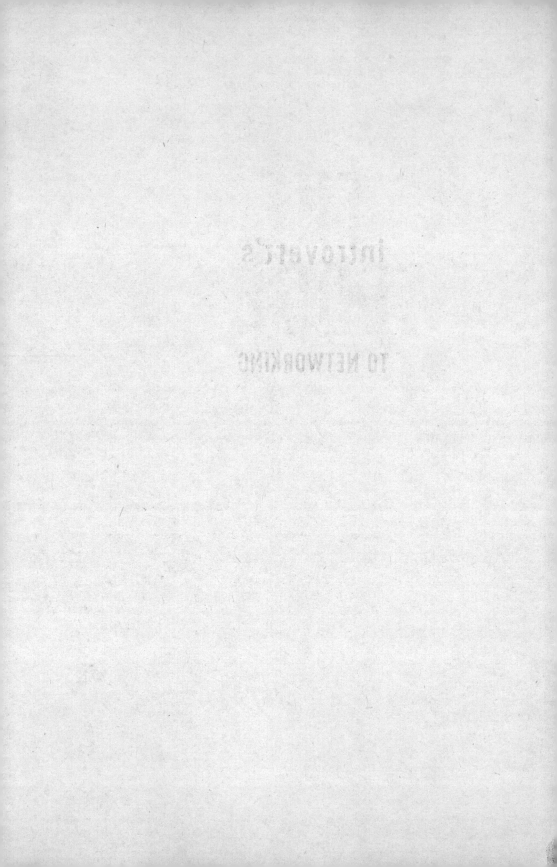

MATTHEW POLLARD

WITH DEREK LEWIS

THE introvert's EDGE

TO NETWORKING

Work the Room, Leverage Social Media, Develop Powerful Connections

HarperCollins
LEADERSHIP

An Imprint of HarperCollins

Published by HarperCollins Leadership,
an imprint of HarperCollins Focus LLC.

Any internet addresses, phone numbers, or company or product information printed in this book are offered as a resource and are not intended in any way to be or to imply an endorsement by HarperCollins Leadership, nor does HarperCollins Leadership vouch for the existence, content, or services of these sites, phone numbers, companies, or products beyond the life of this book.

ISBN 978-1-4002-1671-0 (TP)
ISBN 978-1-4002-1669-7 (eBook)
ISBN 978-1-4002-1668-0 (HC)
ISBN 978-1-4002-2491-3 (ITPE)

Library of Congress Control Number: 2020946152

Printed in the United States of America
20 21 22 23 LSC 10 9 8 7 6 5 4 3 2 1

To my Rapid Growth Academy and Intensive students,
who trust me with their businesses and their lives.

It's been my honor to help you achieve your dreams.

Wars are won in the general's tent.

—STEPHEN COVEY

CONTENTS

FOREWORD BY JEB BLOUNT

When the phone rang, I happened to be the one on my team to answer. The person on the other end of the line worked at a nonprofit and wanted some sales training for his team.

"How much is it?" he immediately asked.

"Well, let me ask you a couple of questions first to make sure we're the right fit for each other," I said, artfully dodging the question. "Let's start with this: what is it about the work you do that's so meaningful for you?"

For the next forty-five minutes, I barely said a word. I let him tell me about his passion, his work, and his people. At the end of it, he said, "Look, I have this much money—can you do it for that?"

Without me really doing or saying anything, the prospect went from asking, "How much does it cost?" to "Would you take my money, please?"

We introverts have a natural ability that gives us the edge over extroverts.

And, yes, you read that right. I, Jeb Blount—worldwide sales speaker and trainer, bestselling sales author, and cofounder of the global sales conference OutBound—am an introvert. In a roomful of people, I'm not naturally going around shaking hands. I'm not great in social situations. I don't like large crowds, and I don't like small talk. I like being by myself. In fact, when Matthew and I first met, we joked about how we lead such public business lives but, in private, prefer to live quietly.

In the entire course of my professional sales career, I may have taken two client lunches. I never went golfing, never went with clients to sporting events. I never did anything all the extroverts were doing, and yet I was always the number one salesperson in every position at every company I worked for, breaking previous records and setting new ones, some of which still stand to this day.

What's the secret advantage we introverts have? The truth is, the most important skill in sales, as in networking, is listening. That's something introverts are great at.

The reason I don't come across as an introvert to my customers is that instead of being shy and awkward like a typical introvert, I appear relaxed and confident like a typical extrovert. I'm able to control a situation in which so many people, especially introverts, feel out of control. Sales isn't an extroverted mask I put on. It's a linear system I follow.

This is exactly why I hit it off with Matthew the moment I met him: He takes a systems approach to sales, too, as he showed in his first book, *The Introvert's Edge: How the Quiet and Shy Can Outsell Anyone.* While there are more successful introverted salespeople out there than most people suspect, Matthew was the first one who truly championed what many of us believed, that introverts make the best salespeople! It's about time someone said it: with the right system, introverts can go toe to toe with extroverts and beat them every time.

Now, Matthew has done it again with his next book in *The Introvert's Edge* series, this time on networking. He's taken another area in which most introverts feel completely out of control, and mapped out a step-by-step process that channels our natural strengths and provides a process to overcome our shortcomings. It's a totally different way of networking, created from an introvert's point of view. It doesn't force us to be something we're not. He doesn't tell us to hide our introverted tendencies or "fake it till you make it." Instead, he simply gives us a way to be our natural selves and yet totally dominate the networking room. What an inspiring message for the billions of us introverts out there.

What I love most about Matthew's system is that he shows how success doesn't hinge on the superficial, like speaking more loudly than everyone else, adopting the right body language, or mastering the handshake. Just like he says in his first book, the secret is in the system. You don't need to be charming or be born with the gift of gab. It's in the approach, and in the frameworks that surround and support what happens in the room.

But as all-important as networking success is, this book goes even further. For me, happiness isn't a state of being. It's a state of pursuit. Life is too short to live miserably. *The Introvert's Edge to Networking* is one of those rare books that shows you how to align what you believe is important with what you do to actually earn money. It not only makes you a powerful networker but ensures you truly love doing it.

People pay me to teach them about what I love most in the world. I wish everyone could experience the same thing. This book will show you how.

Jeb Blount
CEO of Sales Gravy and author of *Inked: The Ultimate Guide to Powerful Closing and Negotiation Tactics That Unlock YES and Seal the Deal*

1

why introverts make better networkers

Failure is simply the opportunity to
begin again, this time more intelligently.

—HENRY FORD

You'd rather get a root canal than go to a networking event.

But you know you're supposed to, right? Everyone says how important it is in landing that dream job, securing your next client, or connecting with a high-level contact who could launch you into the stratosphere. You know you should do it . . . but it's just agony.

Then something happens. Maybe you hear about potential layoffs. Maybe you look up from your work and realize you don't have any customers in the pipeline. Whatever the precipitating event, it takes something seriously scary enough to make that pain worthwhile, to get you out of your comfort zone and into the networking room.

So you decide that, yes, you have to go networking. You go online and find an upcoming event and say, "All right, I can do this." You put it on your calendar. It hovers there for days. Part of you is freaking out: "No, I don't want to go!" Then another part yells back, "You have to!"

There's a feeling of dread as you park your car and reluctantly head into the event. As you walk into the room, your eyes desperately dart around for a familiar face; even though you're trying to expand your network beyond the people you already know, it's far less daunting than approaching a stranger. All the while, you're thinking, "What if no one likes me? What if this is a complete waste of my time? What if I say the wrong thing?" It's like the first day of school all over again.

Failing to see anyone you know, you muster your courage, take a deep breath, and approach the first person you see. Walking toward them, you feel your nervousness take hold. You shake hands and smile courteously. Then you go through the awkward song and dance of introducing yourself: "Hi, I'm Jane Smith. Oh, John Doe? Nice to meet you. What do you do?" You stand there, listening for an indicator that they are the person you're looking for. You're desperate for a new lead on a job (any job) or a new client (any client).

He responds with, "Nice to meet you, too, Jane. I sell insurance. I would love to talk to you about your insurance needs."

Ugh. You didn't come to talk about insurance! "Oh, I think I'm good on insurance, but thank you!" Now it's awkward until John Doe asks what you do. "Thank you for asking. I'm a business coach/accountant/managed service provider."

"Hmm, I already have a coach/accountant/managed service provider I'm happy with."

That's when you think, "Of course you do, so why did I come to this stupid thing in the first place?" Now what? Do you try to tell him why you are better? Try to hustle him away from the person he just said he's happy with? You don't want to feel like you're shoving something down his throat. Perhaps you take the other path, somewhat desperately asking, "Do you know anybody else who might need a coach/accountant/managed service provider?"

John Doe says, "I can't think of anyone off the top of my head, but I'll keep my ear to the ground! In the meantime, can I give you my card in case you change your mind about your insurance needs?"

You don't want his card, but you take it to be polite. You know he's not going to change his mind either, and he wasn't really who you wanted to connect with in the first place. But you hold out hope that, somehow, this encounter will magically turn into a lead.

What do you do now? You've both done the song and dance. You both realize there's no reason to go any further with the conversation. Neither of you wants to look like you're there only to hunt for your next lead—that would be rude. So you smile, one of you makes up an excuse about going to the bathroom or grabbing something to drink, and the other sighs in relief.

Then you have to do the same thing all over again.

Many networking books out there tell you to set a target, such as speaking to five people before you can go home. Perhaps you force yourself to go through the motions four more times. But, of course, those conversations are just like the first. You find yourself wondering, "Why do people say networking is important? I've just wasted half my day!"

After two hours of sheer torture, you go back to your office to lick your wounds and deposit the stack of business cards received, putting them with all the others you've collected over time—all the people you're supposed to follow up with but never do. You probably can't even remember what you spoke to them about. The only thing you know is that you didn't connect with the people you needed to, so why even present the product, secure the sale, and quickly move on to the next house. They could afford to "churn and burn." In fact, to meet their quotas, they thought they had to. Salespeople didn't need to worry about selling inferior goods—or anything else for that matter—because in just a couple of days, they'd be off to the next town, doing it all over again.

What does this have to do with networking?

The same factors that led to a churn-and-burn mentality were re-created in the networking room, as more and more people moved from sparsely populated rural areas into densely populated cities. After all, even today, in many major cities, you'll probably never again see the person you're networking with.

It's why networking, as most people do it today, feels more like door-to-door sales, walking from person to person with a focus on selling as much as possible, as quickly as possible. Creating a meaningful, lasting relationship comes in as a distant second, if at all. This standard approach is what I call "transactional networking." Is it any surprise that it feels inauthentic and even sleazy?

Thankfully, there are those who reject this approach and who do want to create true connections. But they practice what I call "aimless networking." While they may come from a more authentic place, their unstructured approach isn't any more effective than transactional networking. It still results in a lot of small talk, shallow connections, and few successes.

No wonder introverts hate this type of networking so much—me included! This is the exact opposite of how we like to operate. If I had to participate in transactional networking, I couldn't live with myself. If I were an aimless networker, I'd bother? You get back to work, already behind because you spent half the day networking.

I say "spent," but the real word there is "wasted." You're no closer to a good business connection than you were yesterday. You're actually worse off because you spent money on gas and the admittance fee, gave up your time, and severely drained your mental and emotional energy.

You rationalize that your failure is because you're an introvert. After all, the extroverts you saw around the room looked like they were doing great. They must be locking down deals and promotions all the time. If only you could network like them.

But you believe that's not possible for you.

So you convince yourself, at least for now, to endure.

Two or three months later, things take a turn for the worse. In desperation you think, "I have no choice; I need to go back and network." You decide that, this time, you'll do better. You go online and read some networking tips and strategies.

You try one or two of the tips, but networking is still as awkward, painful, and wasteful as before. The experts' advice doesn't make it any more bearable. To you, networking feels like trying to be someone you're not. Sure, it's easy for the extroverts, but networking makes you feel like an introverted square peg forced into an extroverted round hole. You feel sleazy and inauthentic, and you hate small talk! "I guess I just don't have what it takes," you tell yourself.

I've been there. For introverts like you and me, if we're willing to push ourselves to do it at all, networking like this is torture. It's not what we got into our chosen profession to do. We just wanted to earn a great living, doing work we love that revolves around our families and our lives—not spending our days, evenings, and even weekends fake-smiling and engaging in inauthentic, exhausting self-promotion.

HOW DID WE GET INTO THIS MESS?

In her groundbreaking book for introverts, *Quiet*, Susan Cain reminds us that in 1790, only 3 percent of Americans lived in cities. By 1840, it was 8 percent, and by 1930 it was a little more than a third.

In a sparsely populated rural area where everyone knew everyone else, your reputation was everything. As more and more people moved to the cities, however, those community networks became less and less relevant to daily life. As Cain notes, self-help books went from being about inner virtue to being heavily focused on outer charm.

At the same time, due to the Industrial Revolution, factories were producing more goods than their local markets could handle, so they sent salespeople throughout the country peddling their wares. Before this, sales usually happened within the local community. You knew the person you were buying from; merchants, dentists, and others couldn't afford to be known as dishonest or manipulative.

Traveling salesmen didn't need to worry about their reputations, as *Harvard Business Review* suggests in the article "Birth of the American Salesman." They didn't create meaningful relationships with anyone they met, because they were doing business with complete strangers. These salesmen had a short window of time to introduce themselves, get into the house, quickly see that it was a complete waste of time and stop networking altogether.

So, how can we compete with extroverts, who seem to have natural charisma, the gift of gab, and the ability to effortlessly form connections? How can we succeed at networking while feeling authentic?

I'm here to give you good news. Introverts can outperform their extroverted counterparts by realizing two truths:

1. The introvert's road map to success doesn't look like the extrovert's. We're different and we need to embrace that.
2. Traditional networking doesn't work for introverts. We need a smarter approach that leverages our natural strengths.

For introverts, effective networking doesn't look like traditional networking at all. In fact, what I've learned, experienced, and taught is that introverts have a natural edge when it comes to the way networking should really be done—not playing a numbers game and talking to as many people as possible but by being strategic, being prepared, practicing, and knowing how to cultivate deeper relationships with just a few of exactly the right people in the room.

In other words, by playing a totally different game.

This is timely because the old way of networking is quickly becoming obsolete. People can learn all about you, read reviews on the products you sell, see your personal affiliations, learn your employment history, and sometimes even check up on what you did last weekend, all from a phone they carry in their pocket. We're returning to those days when everybody knew everybody—or at least living in a world where people can get a great synopsis, quickly. It's almost impossible to be transactional and then return to obscurity. Transparency is becoming the norm, either by choice or necessity, for individuals as well as employers. Authenticity and inner virtue are back on the rise.

Finally.

STOP COPYING THE EXTROVERTS

Instead of trying to show you how to network like an extrovert, I want to show you how to sidestep that self-destructive behavior. I've discovered a way of networking that leverages our introverted strengths. It allows us to walk out of every room feeling like we've made powerful connections, portrayed the best version of ourselves, and remained authentically "us" the whole time.

Before we go any further, you should know that what I'm about to share with you will require a commitment of anywhere from several hours to a few days of planning, preparation, and practice. One thing I know about introverts, though, is that we're willing to put in the work to obtain a consistently successful outcome, especially when the alternative is more lost time and energy while obtaining near-zero results.

The two types of networking we discussed earlier are not only wrong, but harmful. The transactional approach is purely about onetime deals. I'm sure you don't think of yourself as a selfish person, but this type of networking is inherently self-centered. It's like speed dating, quickly going through as many people as possible until you find someone who'll give you a chance. Put another way, you're trying to get through all the nobodies as quickly as you can until you can find someone you can use to get what you want. To make matters worse, everyone you're speaking to knows this is what you're doing! Sure, you might get a few sales or opportunities, but think about the last time someone behaved this way toward you. Didn't it feel shallow and slimy? That's not the taste I'd like to leave in anyone's mouth, and it's definitely not the path to a higher income and a supportive network.

Aimless networkers, on the other hand, generally walk out with a good feeling, having had some friendly conversations that, unfortunately, ultimately lead nowhere. They may have cultivated acquaintances, but they've created a network that has very little motivation to help them toward their goals. They drift through networking, hoping that, somehow, something good will come from their efforts. It's like throwing quarters into a slot machine, hoping one day to win the jackpot.

However, there is a third type of networking, "strategic networking." It's a smarter and more effective style, one that introverts can dominate. Network strategically, and you will be rewarded with connections to people who value your work and who would love to help you reach your goals faster. It's your ticket off the hamster wheel.

CHANGING THE BALANCE

I discovered strategic networking when I moved across the globe to Austin, Texas, where I didn't know a soul except Brittany, now my wife. While in Australia, I enjoyed a moderately sized network I'd spent a lifetime awkwardly fostering. In my new home, I was confronted with creating a new network totally from scratch.

So I set out on a journey of discovery to make networking easy, fun, and profitable. More than that, I set upon discovering a system that would leverage my introverted strengths, allow me to feel authentic, and give me the edge over my extroverted counterparts. Along the way, I learned something profound: networking, just like with sales, is a system that can be learned and improved upon by anyone, anywhere. Better yet, done well, you can change the balance. Instead of feeling like you're forcing something on people that they didn't ask for, you can get them asking questions because they're genuinely interested.

Going from push to pull was everything for me.

With the right system and process, I don't need to be funny, competitive, or gregarious. When it comes down to it, 90 percent of networking success (at least the way I do it) happens outside the room. I focus on strategy and preparation, not on trying to be charismatic and energetic.

My system ensures that introverts, if they're willing to do the prep work, easily have an edge over their extroverted counterparts. Naturally outgoing extroverts can walk into a room and just wing it. While it often comes off as transactional, they're usually unwilling to put in the time and effort my process requires. After all, they've made it this far on their own—why fix something that they don't see as broken? Introverts, on the other hand, love being superprepared and equipped for success before they ever walk into the room. In the long run, my introverted clients far outperform their extroverted peers because they stick to the process—one that allows their natural gifts, such as active listening and empathy, to shine.

While what you're about to learn will require work, if you put in the effort, it can change your life in a matter of weeks, not months or years. In my first book, I talk about how I learned how to systemize my sales process by watching YouTube videos and practicing at home eight hours a day after a full day's work. I share my journey of going from having no business being in sales—being terrified, really—to becoming the top producer in the nation within just six weeks. I wouldn't wish that six weeks on anyone, but I've carried that training with me the rest of my life. What you're going to discover in this book won't require anywhere near that level of intensity, but the idea is the same: put in the work, systemize the process, reap the rewards.

It's hard to get people to stop and spend a few days on strategy and preparation. Either they're desperate to get instant results, or they feel that activity, no matter how frenzied, equals progress. They believe the hustle will make them successful, that all they need to do is work hard enough and the results will automatically appear.

That may work in the short term, but eventually it burns you out. Instead, if you'll spend just a short time learning and preparing each day for just a few days, you'll catapult forward.

Throughout this book, we're going to tackle just about every kind of situation you can imagine, including someone on the brink of losing everything, someone who saw herself as too old, people who felt underqualified, people who said, "I have no charisma," and those who thought they were socially awkward. You're going to read about people who work in careers or run their own businesses, from marketing and consulting to multimillion-dollar companies and enterprise-level organizations. This system has been tried and tested. It works.

But don't take my word for it. Take Charlene's.

YOU'RE NEVER TOO OLD TO NETWORK

After gardening in the Midwest for most of her life, Charlene Westgate moved to Arizona and found herself presented with a new challenge: How do you make the desert bloom? Through a lot of trial and error, talking with locals, and research, Charlene discovered a few truths. One, she couldn't force her will on her garden. She had to work with her newfound arid climate, not against it. Two, she found the challenge deeply fulfilling. Eventually, she taught herself how to create a thriving garden in the Arizona heat.

When she talked to others about her passion, she found that plenty of people wanted to hear about what she'd learned. Realizing she had something special, Charlene quit her full-time job and opened Westgate Garden Design.

After nine months, though, she still hadn't replaced her full-time income. As a matter of fact, she was struggling to make any money at all. It put a strain on her household, and she grew desperate. When she went into networking events, she found that people didn't really get the value of what she did. She explained how she helped create beautiful gardens that thrived in the arid landscape of Arizona. When people heard the words *garden* and *landscape*, they said, "So you're a landscape architect?" Charlene would then say that, no, she didn't hold the required degree. They would look confused and say, "Okay, if you aren't the architect, do you do the landscaping work?" Given her age, obviously she wouldn't be doing the backbreaking labor. Because she didn't fit into one box or another, people didn't get why they should hire her.

It got to the point that, in Charlene's words, "I was willing to take money from just about anyone, doing anything, just to make ends meet. I wasn't even bringing in minimum wage."

"Networking events were awful," she told me. But she didn't know how else to get the clientele she needed, so she kept going. Event after event, she felt more devalued, more underestimated, and grew more frustrated with trying. Her confidence was shot. By the time I met Charlene, she had almost done what, sadly, so many introverted professionals have done in the past: convinced herself that she didn't "have what it takes" to be successful in business. She wasn't too far away from giving up and closing her business for good.

I helped Charlene see that her problem was that she wasn't articulating her value in a way that made her stand out, that inspired interest, and that made her the only logical choice to hire. The real key was that no one knew how to deal with the Arizona climate as she'd learned to. Charlene finally saw that what she did was something no one else could offer—finding a way to create a beautiful backyard oasis harmonized with the arid terrain that nature had provided.

Soon she was back at networking events, armed with well-planned statements, emotionally driven stories, and differentiation-focused messaging (all of which you will learn about in the pages that follow). When asked what she did, Charlene would talk about how she hates seeing people spend fortunes creating an amazing backyard, only to have it die due to a challenging climate that no one, not even the experts, seems to know how to handle. She would then ask if they knew anyone who had a blank backyard because they believed nothing could survive. Or spent money with a contractor, only to have everything die. Of course, this was a quite common issue. She would then share her own gardening struggles when she first moved and how she learned to harmonize everything with the terrain. Then she'd explain how she used to have a full-time job but gave it up to focus on her lifetime mission of helping people have the same backyard oasis she enjoys every day. Finally, she'd tell a preplanned story of someone she'd worked with in the past, the person's struggles getting anything to grow, and the amazing outcome she delivered. Well, by the end of that, even listeners only partly interested in their backyard couldn't help thinking, "Oh, wow—I want that!" I know the first time she explained it to me, I sure did!

All the previous objections around landscape architects and contractors didn't even come up. Price also didn't seem to matter. Soon she found herself being asked to speak at events, and business boomed.

Originally, Charlene just hoped to earn a decent income doing what she loved, and to surprise her husband with a trip to the Alamo. Today, she's far exceeded her income expectations, won two prestigious small-business-of-the-year awards, and received an unsolicited invitation to appear on local television. All this, just about twelve months after getting ready to close her business forever.

All because she found an effective, authentic way to network.

To use Charlene's words from a recent interview we did together, "This just proves you're never too old to create your dream business."

"Okay, Matthew," I hear you say, "good for her. You love small businesses and you helped a small business. Hooray. But I have a full-time job. How does this apply to me?"

Ask yourself, what if Charlene was an employee of a landscaping company, instead of in business for herself? She could have easily applied the same networking process to help her employer bring in new clients. Don't you think her boss would be ecstatic with that and consider giving her a pay raise?

Or what if Charlene weren't customer facing? What if she were to create a reputation inside the company for specializing in backyard oases that survive the Arizona heat? Do you think that she might be promoted or entrusted with the most high-profile clients' backyards? How long would it be before other companies were coming to her for advice and even trying to hire her away?

But we don't have to guess what would have happened to Charlene. We can look to Justin's example.

NETWORKING SUCCESS AS A BANK EMPLOYEE

When I first met Justin McCullough, he was Capital One's VP of E-Commerce and National Small Business. He'd been a corporate employee all his life, except for one business that left him horribly in debt. In fact, he'd just finally finished paying it off. At Capital One, he specialized in marketing to small businesses through customer-centric initiatives, just as he had in all his past positions. He loved that he got to help small businesses within his job. The problem was, he didn't like working for such a big corporate machine, hated that his job took him away from his family for more than half the year, and felt unchallenged by his day-to-day tasks. He was passionate about having a greater impact on a wider number of businesses and was determined to be around more to watch his two boys grow up. He decided it was time to go into business for himself again and launch his own consulting practice.

Like many incredibly brilliant people who come to me for help, his biggest problem wasn't ability but explaining his value in a way that didn't overcomplicate things. To simplify it, the best Justin could come up with was that he helped people obtain customers and drive loyalty through customer-centric experiences. I first pointed out that "customer-centric experiences" to the average business owner sounded like a cost, not a way to quickly grow their customer base. The verbiage might interest some people, but it wouldn't prick up ears in a networking room. Plus it spoke to the work—where most people get stuck—as opposed to the true value Justin provided. Instead, I suggested he focus his message on the concepts of growth, speed, quick results, and so on. Then he could further hone his message to being the architect or catalyst of such growth via customer centricity.

I then helped him discover three stories from his past experiences, from both employment and from his own small business, to use in networking events to explain the power of what he offered. Armed with that, and the planned networking process we will be sharing in the chapters to come, he was ready to successfully network as an introvert.

But before Justin could put all his hard work into action, tragedy struck his home of Orange, Texas, in the form of Hurricane Harvey. The flooding was catastrophic, destroying more than a hundred thousand homes. Justin and his family vividly remember wading out in waist-high water and climbing into the back of a giant, canvas-back truck to be rescued by the National Guard and taken to a local church shelter.

They lost everything. And while he had insurance, it didn't account for the months of cleanup that bled his business startup fund and personal savings dry.

Understandably, he didn't want to launch a business in a disaster zone while his family picked up the pieces of their lives. What they needed was stability, time to heal, and a new city for a fresh start. He decided that he would put his dreams on hold, leave his family behind, travel to Austin, and do everything he could to obtain employment—quickly, so his family could join him.

No one could blame Justin for being in panic mode: the stress of losing all your possessions, the uncertainty of the future, the pressure to provide, tapped out savings, living miles from his family, and no end in sight until he landed a job. No one would fault Justin's "spray-and-pray," shotgun approach. He called every recruiter, went to every networking event, and told everyone he met that he was looking for a job. But the way he presented himself put him into the commodity box of being just another "marketing executive." At networking events, potential employers would ask about his background, which led to a conversation about Hurricane Harvey and losing everything. While people genuinely sympathized with his plight, nobody wanted to hire a guy looking for a job just because he was desperate and had few options.

A few weeks into this phase of his life, I called to check on him. He shared his struggles of landing a decent job. I asked him, "Justin, what are you telling them?" After he'd recounted his experiences, I saw that he'd completely put his message, passions, and powerful explanatory stories aside. He said that he didn't think it would work for getting a job.

"How is what you're doing today working for you?" I asked. "It's not. It's time to own who you are, Justin. You are passionate about business growth through customer-centric experiences. Put that on your resume. You also told me that you felt motivated to provide value to a wider number of businesses. Did you know many big corporations are in fact an amalgamation of multiple midsized businesses? Why not also add to your resume that you'd be an ideal fit for an organization needing help across multiple business units?

"Next, I want you to understand that networking for a job is exactly the same as networking for new clients. You're still trying to stand out and establish long-term relationships with people. The only difference is, you're doing it to land one long-term 'customer' instead of several. So when networking, and in your interviews for that matter, make sure to introduce your differentiation-focused messaging and use your stories to show your in-depth knowledge and value."

For anyone who hasn't gone through this grueling process, an executive-level hire is no small feat. In fact, it's one of the riskiest things a company can do. But after Justin went back to embracing his uniqueness, he landed three strong offers by networking and interviewing as an interesting outlier instead of someone who just checked the boxes for the job posting. One of those offers was from Facility Solutions Group, an almost $1 billion commercial lighting, electrical, and energy products and services company with multiple small and medium-sized business units operating under its umbrella. At the interview, Justin shared his stories and passion for helping multiple business units grow through customer-centric experiences. Finally, the interviewer said, "You know, Justin, I think you're overqualified for this position, but man, I just know our CEO would love to meet you and hear your ideas. Can you come in tomorrow to meet him for an hour?"

What was supposed to be a one-hour meeting with the CEO lasted for five hours. Then they met for an additional two days, discussing different ways to work together that would make the most of Justin's skills and passion. In the end, they created a brand-new position for him as the chief innovation and product officer, two levels above the original job he'd interviewed for and at a salary six figures more than the one he'd been applying for. Even better, the role would have him based mostly in Austin, without the crazy travel schedule required of him at Capital One.

What if Justin didn't own his uniqueness, passion, and stories? In truth, he is an intelligent, talented person and would have landed on his feet. But would he have obtained his dream job, one he now tells me he loves more than working for himself and allows him to spend more time with his family? Probably not. I love seeing Justin's social posts of nights and weekends with his wife and boys. They all look so happy in their new Austin life. That's the power of being the outlier and knowing exactly how to back it up.

It always surprises me when I hear people commoditizing themselves when trying to land a top-shelf job. At those levels, company leaders want to hire someone exceptional who brings a unique perspective to the task. Yet most candidates present themselves the same way, then wonder why they weren't offered the job. That's why it's so important to know how to articulate your difference, inside and outside the networking room.

Even for an entry-level position, who wouldn't want to hire and promote someone who's really thought about their uniqueness and how it would benefit the right employer versus someone else who just goes through the motions? Employers would much rather work with someone who is passionate and focused.

Justin landed a dream job because he had the courage to network in a way congruent with who he was, because he could clearly articulate his value, and because he was willing to trust the process.

NETWORKING OUT OF YOUR HOODIE

I hope you're excited to overhaul the way you network and are ready to transform your business or career as Charlene, Justin, and so many others have. Before we get to that, let me share one last story about why *The Introvert's Edge° to Networking* had to be my second book, and why it's so close to my heart.

One day, a fan reached out to share that I'd helped his son, Joel Turner, make friends at school. Joel had always shown an interest in business books and happened to pick up my first book, *The Introvert's Edge®: How the Quiet and Shy Can Outsell Anyone*, from the family coffee table. After reading it, he decided that if conversations that resulted in sales could be systemized, then maybe conversations that resulted in friends could too. His dad told me that Joel actually walked around school with my book in hand as he taught himself how to make friends.

I was fascinated and delighted by this story and wanted to speak to Joel myself.

He told me that he used to hide under his hoodie and hated making eye contact but desperately wanted friends. He felt so lonely and excluded. After putting my book to use, he started a dialogue with some of the popular kids. He began feeling like he was in control of the discussion. He began making friends, then getting into more activities. Now there's even a girl in the picture! Today, the hoodie is off for good. (I think it goes without saying how proud his father is of him.)

Joel had gone from being withdrawn to now confident and excited about going to school. What a change! All from grasping that making new friends and connections could be a system.

THE INTROVERT'S EDGE® NETWORKING SYSTEM

So how do you go from an awkward and uncomfortable networker to a networking powerhouse like Charlene, Justin, and even Joel? Well, the answer, as I mentioned earlier, lies in the three Ps: planning, preparation, and practice.

We're going to kick off the steps to this process in chapter 2 by channeling your superpower: your passions. Essentially, we're going to connect a deep-seated sense of purpose to your professional networking aims. While it may sound too good to be true, this will tap into an endless well of energy that will make you want to network. Shortly before writing this, I saw a Facebook post from Charlene saying she was excited about heading out to a networking event. Wouldn't you love to feel like that?!

Chapter 3 is about niching, which may seem odd to include in a networking book. After all, this is about how to connect with people, not do a market segmentation analysis, right? But, just like Justin, you need to accept that success doesn't come from being everything to everyone but being the only logical choice to a select few.

Chapter 4 is about harnessing the power of story. I'll talk about the hard science behind why stories are a better vehicle of communication than just reciting facts and why they're a powerful tool in rapport generation. These aren't your typical business case studies; you'll discover how to create emotionally charged stories that articulate your value and that position you as the only logical choice.

Chapter 5 shows you how to uncover the secret to instantly evoking interest, setting yourself apart, and changing the balance of networking conversations for good. No more will you feel like you're shoving what you do down people's throats. Instead, they'll be asking for more details because they're genuinely interested. This is the crown jewel of my networking system and was the turning point in my own networking journey as well as many of my clients'.

In chapter 6, I introduce the idea that beyond prospective employers or prospective customers, there are two other, more important types of people you want to network with. I'll also show you a simple trick I uncovered to identify, categorize, and even start a discussion with attendees before even walking into the networking room. Get ready to feel the pressure dissipate as we transition networking from a series of first-time meetings to a series of preplanned discussions.

In chapter 7, I tell you exactly what to say when you get in the room. I show you how to plan your discussions so that the conversation goes just where you need it to. Then I present the three different results you want to have with the three different types of people identified in chapter 6, leaving them wanting more and providing them an easy way to get it.

In chapter 8, we'll discuss what to do after you leave the room. You'll put an end to the pile of cards on your desk and, instead, turn them into introductions, deals, and media. No more guessing what to do. No more awkward callbacks. I'll show you exactly how to get your ideal prospects to chase you.

Chapter 9 is about having the right mind-set for the entire process—seeing it as a system to be continually improved upon, rather than a one-and-done effort. I liken it to an assembly line such as Henry Ford's. His brilliance was in continuous improvement. That's the key to your networking success too—perfecting the process.

In the final chapter, I'll show you how your hard work in perfecting your networking system locally will become the catalyst to networking globally. All through the power of technology, psychology, and strategy.

The entire goal of this book is to help you master the room . . . so you never have to go back into one (unless you really want to). This book will give you everything you need to implement my system in your networking efforts. And in the bonus material, which I discuss at the back of the book, you'll find a wealth of information to help you fully cultivate your Introvert's Edge®. With this book, and the bonus resources at your fingertips, nothing can stop you from becoming the master strategic networker you were always destined to be.

Now, let's discover the first element of the Introvert's Edge® Networking System: delving into your passion to come up with your mission—a mission that drives everything else.

channeling your superpower

Outstanding people have one thing in
common: an absolute sense of mission.

—ZIG ZIGLAR

Back in 2014, I had the pleasure of experiencing my first American Thanksgiving. An abundance of turkey, sweet potato casserole, and pumpkin pie—what's not to love? The only problem was, I'd accepted two very early morning TV interviews the following day. So as Thanksgiving Day became late Thanksgiving night, I excused myself. Brittany's family, having not seen each other for such a long while, stayed up having a good time, as they should . . . somewhat loudly. After four hours of broken, restless sleep, I got up and headed to the first TV studio for my interview. As soon as that finished, I rushed off to my second.

Which I now see as ridiculous in retrospect—I'd also scheduled a full day of back-to-back interviews with previous clients. So, immediately after my last TV appearance, I drove right over for the shoot. If these were basic discussions, I might have been able to phone it in. But they were in-depth case studies with previous clients (people like Whitney Cole, Jim Comer, and many other success stories you'll meet throughout this book), in front of bright lights and a full video team.

It was vital that I asked the right questions, kept them on track, and ensured each interview was fluid and instructive. To do this well, it was of paramount importance I stay focused. This was no small task, even if I was fully rested; at a shoot like this, there are a million distractions behind the scenes. At one point, one of the cameramen was even doing yoga right in my line of sight.

I should have been exhausted, but instead it was me pushing the camera team along, all of whom were running on far more than four hours of broken sleep. By the end of the shoot, you could tell that they couldn't wait to pack up and go home while I, on the other hand, was still exploding with energy and having the time of my life. Where did my energy come from? Why was I excited while everyone around me couldn't wait to call it a day?

In a word—passion. I am passionate about helping introverted small-business owners get off the everyday hamster wheel of struggling to find interested prospects, set themselves apart, and make the sale, all while competing against more established businesses in their industry, with prospects who seem to care about only one thing—price. I am on a mission to help them understand that if they focus on just a few things outside their functional skill, they really can have rapid growth in a business they love.

The early-morning TV interviews provided a way I could further that mission. Even though I was exhausted, I found myself charged up and ready just before we went live. As for my day of client interviews, I knew these videos would provide huge value to struggling small-business owners. I also knew that many people would see themselves in these client stories and know that success was possible for them too. It was my passion that drove me. The result: I had plenty of energy on a day when I should have had none.

While this isn't a networking story, it speaks to channeling my superpower. Before I walk into a networking event, I remind myself of my passion and mission, and bang!—I'm ready and excited to get into the room. French general Ferdinand Foch said, "The most powerful weapon on earth is the human soul on fire." Could you imagine if networking were like that for you? Can you see yourself being so excited about sharing your impact that you bubble over with enthusiasm? Being the person so passionate about your work that complete strangers hang on your every word? That your words are infectious and filled with conviction?

By the time you work through my process, that's how networking will be for you—an experience where you seem to have boundless energy, focus, and charisma. Your time in the room will fly. It will be like you uncovered a superpower that's been lying dormant all this time. When you return home, you'll be spent but triumphant. That's what comes from aligning your networking aims to be authentically congruent with who you are and those you want to serve. To adapt the words of American businessman Thomas J. Watson, to be successful, you have to have your heart in your work and your work in your heart. When you speak about something you really care about, you can't help speaking with passion and excitement.

Sadly, few people will ever know passion like this, or the success it can afford them. Not because they don't have passion. Everyone gets excited about something. It's because they've never taken the time to find it and channel it into what they do.

Once we find your passion—the "superpower" that will drive you—we can channel that into your networking efforts. You won't dread networking, you'll love it! I'm not saying that you won't be exhausted afterwards. But it will be a good exhaustion, like the end of a day full of rides and roller coasters at Disney World. These days, that's how it feels for me. As an introvert, the act of networking tires me out, but I get so excited inspiring others with my passion and mission, I don't even notice. I've also now taken the same rides so many times, thanks to my systematic approach to networking, I know all the drops, twists, and turns. Nothing surprises me. I get to just sit back and enjoy it.

DO WHAT YOU LOVE, LOVE WHAT YOU DO

I like to think about strategic networking like getting a rocket ship into orbit. Each element of your rocket ship forms a part of your greater networking system. To extend upon this analogy, if your networking system is your rocket, then passion is undoubtedly the fuel.

This is why uncovering what you're truly passionate about and aligning it with what you currently do, or want to be doing, is vital. Without passion, while you will still be able to portray the most authentic version of yourself and likely still skyrocket your results, you'll always feel incongruent in the networking room. As such, you'll be missing the explosive force you need to truly get to orbit.

I learned this lesson the hard way. Despite my early accomplishments, being responsible for five multimillion-dollar business success stories before the age of thirty, what many people don't know is that much of my success didn't make me happy.

I vividly remember the day I was presented with Melbourne's Young Achiever Award. I should have been ecstatic. After all, I was a kid who, due to my reading disabilities, had been told many times I'd never amount to anything. And there I was, being recognized with a prestigious award for founding what grew into the largest independent brokerage for business-to-business mobile phones in Australia. But instead, I went home that evening to my gorgeous 270-degree city-view apartment and felt . . . just awful.

I'd spent years pushing myself to do things, pushing myself to succeed. Sure, I'd made some great money, but what was it all for? I was more than unsatisfied. I was deeply unhappy. I've been saying for years now that I can create rapid growth out of anything. But there is nothing worse than rapid growth with customers you can't stand in a business that you hate. The same is true for career professionals. Why would anyone want to spend half their waking hours with a boss they can't stand in a job they don't love?

If you hate what you do, no amount of networking strategy and insights are going to make up for the fact that you fundamentally don't want to be doing what you're doing, working toward a goal you don't really want, meeting people you don't really care to know. Networking success starts with finding what sparks excitement in you, then connecting it with what you currently do or want to be doing. If you have that—if you're networking from a place of passion—you're already miles ahead of your competition.

So many people believe that they can't have their cake (pursuing their passion) and eat it too (making a great living). Too many people hate where they spend half their waking hours, living for the weekends or finding enjoyment outside their professional lives. In this chapter, we want to peel back the layers to find something that sparks the fire in the core of your being.

What surprises me most is, for many, their passion is indeed related to what they've been doing all along—they just never spent the time connecting the dots.

Let me explain by showing you how Nick found his fire.

THE BULL-RIDING INSURANCE SALESMAN

Nick Jensen was an ex-bull-rider-turned-insurance salesperson. (You can't make this stuff up.)

When I first met him, he was a mile away from connecting his passion to his day-to-day job. I said to Nick, "Introverts can't just go to a networking event and say they sell insurance. Not only are insurance salespeople seen as a dime a dozen, but they already have a reputation for being overly direct and pushy. If you introduce yourself this way, they'll run for the hills. Extroverts play this transactional numbers game, but we can't. Instead, you need to hook people with your passion and mission."

Nick was such a reserved and logical person that speaking from the heart wasn't really his thing, as is true for most introverts. That said, I've found that while many introverts may struggle to articulate their feelings, inside them lies a river of deep emotion.

So I challenged him: "Nick, you are clearly a very bright man. You could have chosen any path in life. Why did you choose insurance?"

He said, "Well, I just like to protect people, I guess."

"But why insurance specifically? I mean, you could protect lots of people in lots of ways."

Nick said, "I picked insurance because I see so many people earn good money but never really stop to think through what to do with it. Then, something goes wrong, like they get sick or even die, and their family ends up with nothing."

Then I asked him what kind of people he liked helping. Was it just anyone? He said yes, but I challenged him further. Did he like helping a person who earned $500,000 a year as much as someone earning $50,000 a year? Nick said yes, but that the person earning a half-million could pay him more. We weren't getting anywhere with trying to find a connection to his passion.

I said, "Okay, let's not focus on income. What about people who study hard every day to get their dream job, then do the hard work to get promoted to the top spot—versus the person who believes in themselves enough to start their own business and hustles every day to create something. Which of these people do you care about protecting more?"

"The business owner, I think," Nick said. When I asked why, he explained, "I feel like they just deserve my help more."

Again, I asked: "Why?"

"Well, I watched my grandpa work tirelessly on his farm to make it a success. He also employed others, allowing them to look after their own families and save for retirement. But my grandpa never prioritized retirement for himself, and he ended up with nothing. After some farming and health hardships, I had to watch my grandpa sell the farm and move into a tiny house in town. I still remember watching as this once incredibly motivated man just withered away in front of his TV—totally depressed."

"But, Nick," I said, "how could insurance have helped your grandpa? He didn't die. Would life insurance really have made that much of a difference?"

Nick explained that he had spent a chunk of time researching policies to help people like his grandpa. While doing this, he'd discovered a specific type of insurance policy that allowed a business of high cash flow but average profit to leverage that cash into higher-than-average returns. He went on to explain that these policies can allow business owners to propel their gains into real wealth, while still retaining easy access to the cash if and when they needed it. I was blown away by Nick's detailed knowledge. In short, his grandpa could have easily gone into his golden years with quite a bit of wealth. "I like helping these people leverage high cash-value policies so they don't end up like my grandpa. I never want to see people get stuck like that," he said.

I asked Nick how it would feel to wake up every day to help these business owners make sure they never wound up depressed and withering away in their own unhappy retirement—and to ensure that their families were never left with nothing.

He replied, "Wow, that would be amazing!"

"Now let me ask you this: How much easier would it be for you to talk about this passion of yours—this mission of yours— for helping business owners, the hustlers of the world, make sure they end up living the retirement they deserve? How easy would it be to explain that you've discovered a specific product that allows them to leverage their high cash flow into real wealth, while ensuring that they could access the cash whenever needed? Wouldn't that be so much more effective than simply saying you sold insurance?" I asked.

"Absolutely!"

Today, Nick not only gets in front of more prospects than he ever did before, but they are more often the exact people he wishes to serve. When he meets with people in the networking room, they're actually excited to be speaking with him. He also makes much higher sales commissions and, because he's now such a high performer, he lets his family life dictate the hours he works (which he assures me are far fewer than before).

Digging down and finding that spark, then connecting it to what he was already doing, set Nick on fire. Today he's piloting his own rocket ship, right on course. And he loves it.

PUT ALL YOUR EGGS IN ONE BASKET

Every now and then, I run into someone who isn't disconnected from his or her passion and mission but who actually has two. You may think that these people are the lucky ones—that if passion is so vital to success, they must be living financially blessed and fulfilling lives. Unfortunately, this is often not the case, as Jim Comer's story explains.

When Jim was a starving actor in New York in the 1970s, he applied for a job writing sales scripts for Avon's three thousand district managers. After three or four years, he was tapped to write a speech for the CEO. He told me that it was a great speech but felt that the CEO butchered it . . . which is why Jim persuaded the executive that he needed coaching on his delivery, likely risking his job to do so. That eventually led to a successful business as a speech writer and coach for more than a decade in Los Angeles.

Unfortunately, when Jim was fifty-one years old, his father suffered a massive stroke. Very shortly after that, his mother was diagnosed with Alzheimer's. Almost overnight, Jim found himself the caretaker of his parents, forced to give up his life in LA, and to move home to Texas.

He was inspired to write a book to help people just like him, *When Roles Reverse: A Guide to Parenting Your Parents*, that sold more than twenty thousand copies and received rave reviews. He started building a second business around speaking about caregiving, on top of relaunching his speech writing and coaching business.

Here was the problem: it was impossible for him to capitalize on a networking opportunity. Sure, he had passion, but his fuel was split between two different rockets, heading in two totally different directions. I gently suggested to him that he had to make a choice. He couldn't be viewed as one of the world's best speech coaches and become a recognized expert on caregiving. His social media feed looked like "Do You Need to Nail Your Next Speech?" followed by "Do You Have Aging Parents?" It was a confusing message, just like his networking efforts.

Take a second to consider how you reacted to the last person who tried to simultaneously discuss two businesses with you. Regardless of how much passion you felt the person had, you must have left the discussion wondering if he or she was really committed to either one.

As you can imagine, Jim didn't want to abandon either effort. While he was struggling to make any money at all, he'd had a lifetime of experience as a speech writer and coach. He'd also spent a lot of time as a caregiver, along with an exorbitant amount of energy writing a book close to his heart.

Jim finally conceded, after going back and forth, that his real passion was as a speech writer and coach. Today, his business is doing better than ever. Not long after he made this tough decision, one bit of focused effort made him $20,000 within just a few hours (more on that later). He absolutely loves his work . . . all because he reconnected to his true passion and focused all his efforts there.

LIGHTING YOUR FIRE

To truly succeed in strategic networking, you can't bend yourself to what others want, or even what you mean to sell; they must bend to you. Everything you do has to be authentic to who you are as a person and a professional. That's the only way you'll begin to love networking. But first, as self-proclaimed introvert Simon Sinek outlines in his book *Start with Why*, you need to understand why you care enough to go out and network in the first place. After all, if you don't care, why should anyone else?

Take a moment to head to YouTube and search "Elon Musk Falcon Heavy launch." Look at Elon's reaction. His expression is pure joy. There's no doubt in his mind as to what he's doing with SpaceX. He knows his mission: to put a man on Mars. He knows why: it's the first step toward colonization. He's also made no secret about the reason behind it: to bring back the seed of human civilization in the event of a global catastrophe. (FYI, Elon's also an introvert.)

Almost a half-century earlier, John F. Kennedy's mission and passion to put a man on the moon captured the imagination of the entire nation, and even the world. NASA had a mission that superseded everything else. (By the way, JFK was an introvert, too, just like presidents Thomas Jefferson, Abraham Lincoln, Woodrow Wilson, and Barack Obama.) The people at SpaceX and NASA both knew their mission and were inspired deeply by their leaders' passion. That knowledge, catalyzed by the unwavering conviction of their leaders, propelled them to get out of bed every day and hit the ground running. It still propels the team at SpaceX, who after celebrating the momentous step of Falcon Heavy's launch, went right back to work on the next big step.

Introverts who know their mission, and more specifically their passion behind it, feel exactly the same way. It doesn't have to be as grand as a space launch. Like Justin, your mission could be providing customer-centric growth experiences, because you believe a large part of an organization's growth should come from serving current clients. Or like Charlene, whose mission is creating backyard oases that thrive in the Arizona heat because she hates seeing people spend fortunes on backyards that end up dying.

Being connected with your passion and mission gets people to give you their time, money, networks, and ideas. They'll want to follow you, work with you, and help you get where you want to go. This is the kind of stuff that moves mountains.

To get to this place, however, it's time for some introspective thinking. You need to dig deeply into who you are and uncover that spark that has been there all along. You need to explore how you ended up in your chosen profession and how it connects in a way that, like Nick, may not seem totally obvious right away.

To find your rocket fuel, you need to be able to answer three important questions:

1. What do you want to see (happen, stop happening, change, or improve) in the world, within the workplace, with customers, with suppliers, with prospects, and so on?
2. Why do you care?
3. What's the driving passion behind it?

For the moment, don't worry about how you'll make money from your passion, or even how you'll convince your boss to let you pursue that mission. I want you to suspend your logical brain's tendency to cut your dreams off. You've closed this door for so long. Let some fresh air blow through. Give yourself the opportunity to imagine "what if?"

I'm not asking why you are networking. It's probably because you need leads, either for new customers or for a new job. What I'm asking is what's important enough to get you to jump out of bed in the morning, outside of the money you get paid or the worry of making none. Think about leaving your loved ones every morning or being away from them for long periods of time. What's important enough to make that worth it? Imagine yourself in all kinds of tough business and job situations, well beyond simply networking. What's important enough to you to get you through these moments with energy and focus?

If you're like many of my past clients, the answers may not come to you right away. You may even be drawing a complete blank. Don't worry, that's quite common. Try asking yourself some of these questions to get the juices flowing:

▸ I could have done anything—why this (that is, why did I decide on this profession)?

▸ Do I have any personal connection to the business or career I've chosen? Any personal stories that connect me to it?

▸ At work, what do I get my greatest joy from? (Your answer to this question can include previous jobs or businesses.)

▸ What are the tasks that I do that make time fly?

▸ What do I hate seeing happen to (prospects, customers, suppliers, coworkers, and so on)?

▸ What do I love seeing (prospects, customers, suppliers, coworkers, and so on) experience?

▸ What are my favorite types of problems to solve at work?

▸ What do I get the greatest joy from in my personal life? How can I make that relevant in my business or career?

This may be the first time you've even asked yourself these types of questions. It didn't occur to me to ask them of myself until after receiving the Young Achiever Award and realizing I was so unhappy. Until then, I would have seen these questions as totally unnecessary for success. Now, however, I understand that the answers were not only critical to my mental well-being but the catalyst for making great money doing what I love.

So, while you might be tempted to come back to this later, I urge you to pause for a moment and really take the time to answer the above questions—to discover the answers that will change your life for the better.

Just as they did for Tarek Morshed.

When Tarek first came to me, he was a Sotheby's real estate agent looking for an edge. He was good at his job—excellent, in fact—but he was competing with tens of thousands of realtors in the area. Originally, his reason for wanting to obtain a higher sales volume was to be afforded the opportunity to take on a greater leadership role, step away from the day-to-day sales grind, and, of course, earn more money. But going into a networking event and saying, "I want to get your business because I'd love to earn more money or grow my team," doesn't exactly inspire people to want to work with you.

When I originally asked Tarek what he cared about most, it always came down to meeting amazing people and selling homes. "What type?" I asked. "Maybe unique, high-end homes?" But after pushing him, it came out that he took pride in his own home. He loved its central location, making it easy to get to meetings. He loved the way it was set up for work-life balance and how productive it kept him. We went deeper, and soon he was sharing stories about how he had helped senior leaders, CEOs of big companies, and entrepreneurs all find their perfect spaces.

He understood that a home's location was of paramount importance for business owners who worked a significant amount of time from home. He'd point out to these clients that, sure, they could find a bigger or cheaper home farther from the commercial hub, but that the farther out they lived, the harder it would be to network. If an event is forty minutes away instead of ten, you'll be more likely to skip it, despite it being prospect-rich and full of moneymaking opportunities. Tarek also understood how important the location of their home workspace was. Too close to family areas would bring distractions. Lack of natural light and scenery would kill creativity and productivity. Lastly, Tarek knew how important it was to align the purchase of a home with the business's needs. For example, if a client's business was going into growth mode, then the person shouldn't buy a house that was going to require more care and higher maintenance. Nor should such clients buy a more expensive home just when their business was going to need financial resources too.

Tarek's passion quickly became obvious. We retooled his entire brand around helping entrepreneurs, founders, and CEOs of highly successful businesses find their true entrepreneurial home. If you're in Austin and want to buy a house, any realtor can help you. But if you're a founder or entrepreneur looking for a home that works into your vision for your business instead of detracting from it? There's only one person to call.

Tarek even started *The Entrepreneurial Home* podcast on which he interviews top CEOs and successful entrepreneurs about their own home workspaces. This has given him access to some exclusive people who might otherwise have been quite hard to connect with.

All of this came from realizing his passion, crafting his mission, then sharing both with the world.

We've all seen people walk into networking events like soldiers of fortune, trading in more and more of their humanity for a quick buck. That's not the path for you. You can't evoke authentic engagement if you have a singular focus on obtaining a quick win. Your vision has to be bigger than just getting paid well, bigger than just a onetime deal.

It's time to discover who you really are and what you really care about. Sharing this with others is your path to creating authentic and genuine connections. It's your path to creating the types of rich and rewarding relationships that will propel you to your ultimate goals.

In the next chapter, I'm going to show you why success doesn't come from being everything to everyone but being the only logical choice to a select few. Then I'm going to help you discover who that select few should be.

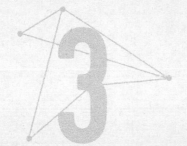

you can't please everyone

If you try to please all, you please none.
— AESOP'S FABLES,
"The Miller, His Son, and the Ass"

When you're desperate for clients, any client is a good client, right? Just like when there are layoffs and you're desperate for a new job, anything sounds better than nothing. So you network with anyone and everyone; after all, you just need one employer or just a few prospects to say yes. But let me ask you this: Do you really want just any job—even one you hate? Do you really want to work with just any client—even a bad one?

To truly succeed at networking, you need to stop casting a wide net and instead focus on being the perfect fit for just a select few.

This is the group that will be motivated to hire you, buy from you, appreciate your work, and pay you what you're worth—the group that sees you as the only logical choice, regardless of your competition.

To this group, there is something singular about you and what you provide. They see something inside you that, perhaps, you don't even see for yourself—yet! It's a mixture of unique personal and professional experiences, the skills you possess (often the ones you take for granted), the way you view the world, how you handle problems, and your passion for getting things done.

Let me explain by telling you about Leslie Hill.

Leslie was a regional VP at the multilevel marketing company Arbonne, which makes beauty and wellness products to promote healthy living. She'd recently moved from Michigan to North Carolina, leaving her entire network behind. Somewhere along the way, she stumbled across my first book and used my advice to create a systematic sales process. In a recent discussion, she told me she'd been having great success. As an introvert, she loved how in control she felt when it came to something that seemed impossible to plan for.

Leslie explained that her biggest epiphany came when she read the last chapter, in which I discuss how much easier sales can be when you first find and focus on a niche. Suddenly, it became clear to Leslie that she'd been going about networking all wrong.

Leslie thought about who she wanted to be working with and who would really see value in working with her. She decided that the perfect fit for her would be healthcare providers—more specifically, medical professionals who understood the importance of nutrition for better health.

Armed with this new focus, Leslie decided to put it to the test. She headed to a local event, hosted by her chamber of commerce. As she walked into the room, she spied one woman in particular who seemed to know everyone. She walked up to the woman, introduced herself, and asked what kind of client she was looking for. The woman shared her ideal client, then reciprocated by asking Leslie the same.

Leslie said, "Medical professionals who 'get it'—who get that nutrition is part of health."

The woman immediately said, "Oh, I know the perfect person you need to speak to—Dr. Mike!"

She then walked Leslie across the room to introduce her to Dr. Mike. After Leslie delivered her prepared remarks (more on that later), Dr. Mike said, "I've been hoping to run into someone like you!" Shortly after that, he booked four workshops with Leslie at his clinic. He also introduced her to another healthcare professional who was so excited about what Leslie did that she, in turn, introduced Leslie to a number of other doctors and healthcare professionals, leading to multiple workshops and speaking opportunities.

Leslie had frequented that chamber event many times before. But this was the first time that, instead of saying, "I'm looking for anybody interested in beauty and wellness products," she got ultraspecific by focusing on nutrition-conscious healthcare providers. So specific that, for the niche that she'd decided upon, she became an easy yes.

To be exciting to a few, you need to exclude the rest.

As another example, take Blackbaud. In the world of online bookkeeping, there is massive competition from the likes of QuickBooks, Xero, MYOB (Australia's largest), Sage, and FreshBooks. They all spend fortunes on new features, marketing, and customer acquisition. Meanwhile, Blackbaud enjoys incredible growth, year over year, fairly uncontested in an otherwise saturated market. How? By understanding that everyone is not their customer and focusing on becoming the gold standard for nonprofits. They don't have to spend a fortune on research and development. They can wait to see what the giants do and adopt best practices into their own products.

Because they know their niche inside and out, and their niche knows them, marketing is simple.

BEYOND YOUR NICHE

Of course, I'm not suggesting that you go and fire all your current clients, quit your current job, or turn down opportunities that come your way just because they aren't in your niche. So often, when discussing the importance of an ideal niche, I'm met with a reply like, "Yes, Matthew, that group would be perfect for me, and I'd love to work with them. But what if I get the opportunity to work with someone outside this niche? Do I have to turn them down?"

I always answer in the same way: "Of course not! You should never turn down any opportunity without at least some consideration. People get niching all wrong. Just because you pick a niche doesn't mean you can't do anything else. It especially doesn't mean you can't work with the people that already know, like, and trust you, or are referred to you by those that do. Our focus with niching is purely on obtaining new prospects and employment opportunities from outside your current customer base or referral network. To focus your energies on being the perfect fit for that select few. That's it!"

As soon as niching is explained to them in this way, their fears subside, and they are ready to jump into their newly discovered niche with both feet.

Another niching misconception is that you must continue to focus only on your niche for all eternity. This feels like a daunting commitment. Let me put your fears to rest: not only have I personally moved from niche to niche but so have many of my clients. As you build momentum within your current niche, you leverage that momentum to expand.

For instance, in the education space, I grew a business to thirty-five hundred business-owner students in just three years. Initially we focused on a specific trade, electricians. Then we grew to serve all tradespeople on a worksite. Then we grew into serving florists and hairdressers. Before we knew it, we were working with doctors and lawyers.

This level of growth would likely not have happened if we'd started by offering business education to everyone. It likely wouldn't have even happened if we started with a focus just on trades. It was that we started with just electricians, and we leveraged that momentum to grow step by step. That's what led us to rapid growth.

The final objection that comes up with niching is this: What if you go to a networking event and share your passion, mission, and niche, and that person doesn't work in that space? What do you do then? Do you quickly hustle to remain relevant or stick to your guns?

You stick to your guns, and here's why: you're about to take networking to a place you've never taken it before. Soon you'll be prepared with a well-structured way of articulating your mission and niche, and you'll be armed with a whole lot of strategic networking gems. You'll find yourself with an infectious charisma that you've likely never experienced before. This newfound enthusiasm means that others get excited about your mission, just like Leslie's new contact. They'll have a colleague, a friend, a coworker, or somebody else who is in your perfect niche, and they'll walk you right up for an introduction.

In fact, I've also found that many people will actually try to bend themselves or their problem to your niche. They often respond with, "Well, I'm not exactly the type of person you described, but we have a lot of the same problems. I think you'd be really helpful in getting us past them. Would you consider doing some work for us?" Think about what a role reversal in networking that is, to go from trying to pitch someone to having them trying to mold themselves to you.

I've had product companies, extroverts, and even billion-dollar tech corporations—all groups outside my target niche—explain to me how my systems and processes could work for them too; they just need someone like me with the passion and skill to make it happen.

It all starts with one small niche. Let's get to work finding yours.

THE BASICS OF NICHING

Discovering your perfect niche is easier than you think. We can find it in just three simple steps.

Before we get started, if you're literally right out of uni (you Americans would say college) or just starting out in a new and vastly different industry, this is your official get-out-of-step-one-free card. Please proceed directly to step two, read that to the end, and at the bottom you'll find customized advice just for you.

Also, this process is slightly different for business owners and career professionals, which is why I've broken step one into two parts. Don't worry, the outcome will be the same.

Step One for Business Owners

First, get out a pen and paper. You're going to make two lists.

On the first list, write down the names of people who, when your phone rings with their number in the caller ID, you hear "cha-ching!" These are high-paying customers who pay you what you're worth and never haggle on price. Or they may be people you've worked with only once, but they were clients who were happy to pay you well for it. This doesn't necessarily mean you enjoyed working with them, only that you made great money for the work you did. You can think of this as your "cha-ching!" list.

For the second list, write down the names of people who sing your praises. This may mean raving to others about your work or products. It could be people who consistently send referrals your way. They're the people who, when you ask for a short testimonial, write you a page. Think of these people as being on your "evangelists" list.

Don't write down just a few names. These need to be exhaustive lists. Put down everyone who's ever paid you well or had a positive interaction with you professionally. (And notice these are all people, not companies. We don't do business with organizations; we do business with the individuals inside them.)

Step One for Employees

You'll still have a cha-ching! list and an evangelists list. The only difference is in the way we define the people who go on them.

For your cha-ching! list, you need to think in terms of both your internal customers and your employer's external customers. (Again, individuals, not companies.) Think of your current and former bosses, direct or indirect managers, and even coworkers as customers. Which of them ensured you were paid your bonuses, gave you generous raises, or otherwise financially rewarded you? Who gave you opportunities that either directly or indirectly led to a monetary benefit? What external customers always wanted to work with you—and when the phone rang with their number on it, your employer heard cha-ching! These people love paying your employer because they get to work with you.

On your evangelists list will be the people always telling others about you and your outstanding work. They recommended you for special projects or awards. They constantly encouraged and supported you in seeking promotions. They worked with you in the past and are very happy to serve as references. Or they know you and your work well through an association or group you're both part of. These are the people who appreciate you, trust you, and go to bat for you.

Step Two

All right, have your cha-ching! and your evangelists lists? From here on out, the process is the same whether you own a business or are a career professional.

Now you need to sort these lists. Look at all the names you've written down across both lists. You'll start to notice some similarities. Whatever you notice, sort them into groups according to those characteristics. This might include wanting help with a specific outcome, like veterans needing career guidance as they reenter civilian life, or CEOs wanting to win an award like Great Place to Work. Maybe they're old-school retailers who want more of a digital presence on social media. It might be bringing systems and processes to their chaotic workday. Perhaps they are partially deaf and want to hear sound clearly when watching TV, or they want to rebuild their strength after pregnancy (yes, these are real niches my clients have uncovered).

Or these groups might be sorted by one or more of the following:

- Demographics: age, gender, marital status, religion, nationality, education, income
- Psychographics: beliefs, attitudes, and guiding principles that prevail when determining how they think and behave
- Geographic: physical location, country, state, city, county, postcode, subdivision
- Behaviors: why people do what they do, the patterns of their lives

It could be that they have specific wants, needs, fears, or problems in common. These might be competing business demands, leadership problems, an unusual plateau in what would normally be a long history of growth, or a particular life event that led to a shift in priorities. I have one client whose niche is all alumni of the same school. Another one's niche is empty nesters looking to build their forever home. Maybe your niche loves musicals or orchestras. Maybe they're working moms or stay-at-home dads. Just as you got exhaustive with the names on your two lists, get exhaustive about coming up with every kind of conceivable way to sort your lists into multiple groups that share characteristics.

Finally, before we move to the next step, a word of warning. Don't make the mistake of disregarding groups with just a few names within them. In the final chapter of my previous book, I introduced Wendy and explained how we discovered her niche based on just two clients.

If you've read my first book, you already know her story, but let me recap. Wendy was a struggling Mandarin-language coach. Like many other markets where there is fierce local and global competition, there were competitors willing to provide their services at a fraction of the price. In an effort to help her sidestep this price war, I noticed one tiny group of two names. Just two names out of the hundreds of clients she'd listed and the dozens of groups we'd sorted them into. As it turns out, they were high-level executives relocating with their families to China. After digging deeper, Wendy revealed that the guidance she provided helped them and their families to thrive in a country with far different cultural norms—something far beyond and far more valuable than strictly language tutoring. That was a niche with nearly zero competition. With just a few strategies, she went from struggling to make $50–80 an hour for private language coaching to making $30,000 per family group for the easiest sale in the world.

All this from a small group we could have easily overlooked. So, while it can seem tedious, I urge you not to overlook or exclude these smaller groups. One of them could be your ticket to a different life.

For Those Just Starting Out

Reading the above, you might be thinking, "Well, those would be two very blank lists." And you'd be right. But when you have zero runs on the board, the last thing you want to do is compete like-for-like against those who have many. This is why it's even more important to specialize right out of the gate.

Sure, if you're an ex-engineer and you've decided to pursue a new career in copywriting, then specializing in copywriting for engineering firms might be a great first niche.

If, on the other hand, you're right out of uni or starting out in a new and vastly different industry, then you'll need to create groups by researching the demographics, psychographics, and behavioral characteristics of groups (for example, possible employers and prospects) that you feel could have alignment with your overall passion and allow you to pursue your life mission (which we uncovered together in the last chapter).

Keep in mind, you likely know little about your potential groups, so I'm definitely not saying you should just jump in blind. You'll want to do everything you can to better understand all your possible options. You could start by checking out podcasts and magazines related to your groups of interest, to see if your excitement grows or dissipates as you learn more about their problems and focuses. You could also check out First Research's list of Industry Profiles, IBIS World's Industry Reports, and any information you can garner from related associations and societies. You can even reach out to a few people who are already working with or for one of the groups you are evaluating and ask them a few questions.

Finally, as you go into this research phase, remember there is also a balance. You could easily spend a lifetime analyzing each possible group. Give yourself an allotment of time, spend that time thoroughly researching your options, then join me in the next section (skipping past step three) to make your choice.

Step Three

Business owners and career professionals, I now want you to get out a red marker. Looking across your sorted minigroups, circle the ones that you've made fantastic money from. Like your original cha-ching! list, these are people who, when your phone rings with their number on it, you're almost assured it's money in the bank. Circle a group only if every person in it is a moneymaker for you or your company. If inside the group many, but not all, names fit this requirement, you may consider niching down even further, using additional criteria outlined in step two, to separate out those that fit with those that do not.

Next, go through your minigroups again, this time with a blue marker, circling the groups who sing your praises. Like your original evangelists list, you know you can rely on these people to support you with referrals and testimonials. Again, circle a group only if everyone in it is a raving fan, and consider niching further if many, but not all, names fit this requirement.

You'll notice some groups have just a red cha-ching! circle around them, which means great money, but they don't show you off to the world. While you'll enjoy a good payday, you risk falling into the trap of work you won't love with customers you eventually won't be able to stand.

You'll also notice a few groups with just a blue evangelists circle around them. They love you and you probably love them, but you need to make money. Even if your mission is to save the world, you won't be doing it very long if you can't afford to eat.

Finally, you'll notice one, two, or even several magical groups, the ones that have both a red and a blue circle around them. One of these groups, and only one, is your target niche for all your networking efforts. (I'll show you how to choose in just a moment.)

It's that simple and that hard. And trust me when I say this: you are going to love working with this group. I mean, who doesn't love people who sing their praises, share their great work with the world, and pay them well too!

MAKING THE TOUGH CALL

As a business owner or career professional, you might have uncovered two, three, or even twenty groups with a red and blue circle around them. If you're right out of uni or just starting in a new industry, you also, hopefully, have identified many groups, with many combinations of characteristics, to choose from. Regardless of how many you have—and here's the important part—you can pick only one. Just like Jim Comer in chapter 2 couldn't pursue two missions driven by two unique passions, you have to select just one group to give your full attention. When you do, amazing things happen—things you'd miss out on if you had a scattered focus, chasing every bouncing ball.

While it's okay, even smart, to hedge your bets when it comes to managing a financial portfolio, when it comes to managing your professional focus, you can't afford to be pulled in two or three or ten directions. As with Jim, you have limited time and a finite amount of energy, and you can't portray yourself as the only logical choice if you have your feet in multiple camps.

Simply put, pick the group that most aligns with your passion and mission. In the long term, that's the one you'll make the most money from and love your life while doing it. Don't be one of those people who settles for a niche because it sounds like the most sensible path. I want to challenge you to pick the group you know in your heart that you're going to love to work with.

Because here's the thing about choosing the "safe" niche: there's always going to be someone who really does love working with that group. Their natural passion and enthusiasm will have them rocketing past you, snatching up leads or promotions faster than you ever will. You might be able to compete with them for a little while, but then one day times will get tough, like the 2008 global financial crisis, COVID-19, or just because something changes in your industry. Without the same rocket fuel as your competitors, you'll soon begin to say to yourself, "What am I even doing this for? This was supposed to be the safe, practical choice. Now it's just as hard as anything else, and I hate what I'm doing! Why did I do this to myself?"

Don't let this be you. Make the tough call.

KNOW YOUR DIFFERENCE

Now that you know your niche, it's time to discover your secret sauce. It's time to answer the question "What are the three main reasons they think you're so fantastic?" In asking this, I'm not talking about the reasons they hired you or purchased your product. I'm talking about the unexpected surprises that make you a standout.

This can often be a difficult question for many introverts to answer. I'm forever hearing people say, "It's easy for me to see the uniqueness in others, but when it comes to myself, I can't really figure it out." Unfortunately, a lot of us introverts spend way too much time focusing on our weaknesses, instead of considering our strengths. We also often overlook or even devalue many of our natural skills and talents, favoring instead the skills and talents that took considerable time to learn.

While there are many ways to uncover the special qualities that make you indispensable to your target niche (you can access these methods in the bonus materials), the best way, by far, is how Jon Harris did it.

Jon was a second-generation printer out of Sacramento, California. Unfortunately, over the last two decades, printing had become just about as commoditized as you can get. How in the world could we create some way to let Jon and his employees introduce themselves as anything other than a print shop offering the same commoditized services as the UPS Store, Office Depot, FedEx Office, and every other printer that showed up on a Google search?

Doing his niche exercise had been easy. The people circled in both red and blue—Jon's evangelists and most profitable customers—were founders of educational training companies. In fact, out of the hundreds of accounts Jon had, two educational training companies in particular generated almost 80 percent of the company's revenue.

"Jon, do you realize what this means?" I asked. Jon said yes—it was terrifying to have his whole business riding on just two accounts. After all, what if one stopped using him?

While he was correct, I had the opposite reaction to the discovery. "Think of it this way," I told him. "If you fired all of your other customers and got just two more like these, you'd double your business!"

When I asked Jon what it was about his two big clients that kept them coming back—especially as he wasn't the cheapest—he answered, "They like our service and find us knowledgeable."

"This is what people always say, but there's always more to it," I said. "There are lots of companies that promise great service and plenty that are cheaper. You need to be thinking what it is specifically about your knowledge and service they appreciate. What you provide that they can't get anywhere else. Because that's what they're thinking about every time they pay your bill or receive a cold email/call from one of your lower-cost competitors."

Sadly, it didn't seem to matter what I asked Jon, or how I asked him; he couldn't seem to find the answers we were searching for.

Eventually, I said, "Jon, you're going to have to pick up the phone and ask them."

Now, you may be thinking, *I'd rather pull my own nails out than have to make this phone call.* But as you might have learned from reading my first book, I like to script these types of interactions, so that you go into the call knowing exactly what to say. You can even practice a little, so that you feel more comfortable before you even pick up the phone.

The script I suggested to Jon went something like this:

"I wanted to thank you for being such a great customer. [Let them respond.] As a matter of fact, I've been working with a new coach"—I always tell my clients to blame me; feel free to do the same—"and when he asked me who my best customers were so he could help me find more just like them, the first name I thought of was yours. It really has been an honor to work with you and your team. I hope you don't mind, but when I said your name, he suggested I call you and ask you why you've been such a loyal client to us."

The initial response is always along the lines of, "Well, we just really love your customer service and how you do business."

I taught Jon to respond with, "[Name], I appreciate that. Thank you so much. Is there something specifically about our service that you value the most?"

By saying "specifically," it makes the person think about some instance or some detail—something that stands out in the person's mind as important. It forced Jon's customers to think about the details rather than what they provided as a generality.

In Jon's case, it turned out that there were three huge benefits that both educational training companies said they found invaluable.

First, anyone in the educational training space will tell you that when you customize trainings for an organization, you're always saddled with last-minute changes. The facilitators conducting these trainings often find themselves running around at ten o'clock at night at their local Staples, reprinting something, then having to stay up to reassemble their workbooks in preparation before their class or flight the following day. Jon's team, on the other hand, did all of that assembling themselves and were used to last-minute revisions. So the facilitators knew all they had to do was send their files to Jon's team and they'd take care of the rest. Avoiding that stress alone made Jon and his team an indispensable asset.

Second, the facilitators had the confidence that Jon would step in as a much-needed fail-safe in the event they missed something in their rush to get it done and off to printing. Jon would always seem to catch something important that the facilitator had missed. After working with educational institutions for years, Jon had a mental checklist of everything a workbook typically needed. For instance, the two things facilitators overlooked most often were a table of contents and page numbers. If you've ever been in a workshop where the workbook was missing page numbers, you know how tedious it gets with the instructor trying to move back and forth between pages and exercises. It frustrates the participants, embarrasses the instructor, and reflects poorly on the organization. Jon's customers came to rely on him to be their "final proofer," allowing them to feel confident that the workbooks were 100 percent perfect, 100 percent of the time. This peace of mind was more than enough to choose Jon and his team over any other printer.

Third, Jon's customers relied on him to arrange the logistics in getting their workbooks to the right conference room, hotel ballroom, or trade-show booth. Most printers would never accept ownership of this complicated task. Facilitators often find themselves taking the material with them, lifting heavy boxes in and out of cars, checking it in as luggage on flights . . . it's a nightmare. Jon just owned the problem. He worked with the shipping companies, always getting a much cheaper price, then confirmed the workbooks had arrived at their destination and been stored somewhere safe. The facilitators never had to worry. Again, more than enough for Jon's best customers to keep using his services.

Putting all three of these specific benefits together, Jon had created a service specialization without even realizing it. To him, it was just the way you were supposed to do business!

Let's stop here to let you reflect on that for a moment. Whatever you do, I promise you're like Jon. You might think that what you do isn't that special, that "I just provide the same thing everyone does." But the way you do it and how you work with clients or employers is unique. It is different. In fact, it's what sets you apart from all the other people out there with your functional skill or product. It's what your customers appreciate and come back for.

Jon just thought he was providing good customer service—and he was. However, what Jon saw as basic good service was what his best customers saw as his competitive edge, the whole reason they worked with him instead of some other, cheaper competitor. In other words, they didn't put him in the same commodity box that he'd put himself in.

So what you need to do is to write down the three higher-level benefits you offer your niche, as Jon did. The things you do above and beyond your functional skill or the product you provide.

By now, there might be a few things that come to mind. That's excellent! Remember, however, that we often have blind spots to the little things—the things that come easiest to you, that you do so naturally, and that make the biggest impact on your niche prospect or potential employer. Which is why, even if you feel 100 percent certain that you have the answers, I still highly recommend picking up the phone to ask.

No one would pay you more than others or continually tout your abilities if you worked exactly the same way as everyone else out there. They wouldn't recommend you for promotions or refer others your way if there weren't something special and different about you. This is the group you circled in both red and blue, so they know exactly what makes you stand out.

For Jon, it was turning around last-minute changes, ensuring nothing was missing, and coordinating delivery.

What about you?

4

we all tell stories

There are two ways to share knowledge.
You can push information out. Or you
can pull them in with a story.

—ANONYMOUS

Bethany Jenkins and her husband, Shan, were luxury custom home builders. They and their team worked with people who wanted that "crown jewel," the $3–$10 million home that blew you away. While networking, they'd run into plenty of people who wanted a home like this, but who would often say, "We're looking for a designer now; we'll reach out to you when we're looking for a builder." Or maybe, "We have a builder we like already; we're just looking for a designer to get it drafted." Bethany and Shan would also try to network with realtors, whose response was generally, "We already have a builder we recommend."

But Jenkins Custom Homes isn't just a builder—it's a design-build firm. The distinction is important. On typical projects, where the design and build are done by separate firms, the two sides rarely communicate well with each other, leading to last-minute chaos and rush from the builder saying, "You need to pick X item, and we need to know your choice today." The builder and designer usually blame each other for cost overruns or flawed planning, forcing the client to play mediator on top of everything else. The stress of it all can take its toll on a marriage, leave customers with a house they resent, and even turn a dream home into a nightmare.

That's why it's so important to work with a design-build company who knows what the extras cost, when selections need to be made (giving notice well in advance), and how to design their client's dream home within budget.

The Jenkins team had a problem communicating this. Bethany felt that no matter what they said, they came off sounding as though they were bad-mouthing the competition—or even trying to scare prospects into giving Jenkins their business—when all they wanted to do was educate people on the benefits of their approach.

As the years went on, Shan decided he could no longer continue to focus on both the construction and sales sides of the organization. But Bethany didn't want to be solely responsible for the networking and sales element of the business either. She didn't want to be the one doing this pitchy, yucky-feeling stuff.

Bethany and Shan decided they were going to have to hire a salesperson. But in an effort to save them the expense, I told Bethany that we could instead create a system for her, one that leveraged her natural introverted strengths. Bethany had always believed that her introverted nature was in direct conflict with networking and sales, but she agreed to trust in my faith in her. She was going to try to do it herself.

"Still," she immediately asked, "how do I not sound salesy in meetings, or at networking events, when people say, 'I've already got a relationship with a designer; I'm just looking for a builder'—or vice versa?"

"Just tell them a story," I said.

"For example, have you ever had a prospect come to you with a designer's plans, only to inform them that the design didn't fit their budget?" Bethany replied that it happens way too often. I asked her to tell me about her worst example.

Bethany told me about the time a prospect, Megan, came into their office, explained what she wanted, then handed over her designer's plans. She seemed like a lovely person, and the discussion was going quite well. In an attempt to conclude a really positive meeting, Shan said, "Great, let us take a look over your plans in more detail and we'll get back to you on a fixed price."

Megan replied, quite anxiously, "Can you just give me a ballpark figure now?" Normally, they would say no, that it takes time to calculate all the costs correctly. But this sweet and reserved woman was quite insistent about getting a number right away. Shan finally provided an off-the-cuff, rough guesstimate. Megan burst into tears.

She told them that she had informed her designer what her budget was. But after getting the plans, she'd gone to four different builders whose prices were double what she'd budgeted. Megan had worked with her designer for two years to plan the home of her dreams . . . and now five builders had told her there was no way she could afford it. She was either going to have to cancel building her home altogether or spend more money to design a lesser home, always knowing it wasn't what she really wanted. "How could this happen?" she cried.

I said to Bethany, "As unfortunate as poor Megan's situation is, it is a perfect story for showing—not telling—people why working with a designer and builder separately is so risky."

Today, when networking, if Bethany meets someone saying, "I've already got a relationship with a designer, I'm just looking for a builder," she simply responds with, "Congratulations on starting the process toward your dream home. What a huge milestone. If you've already locked in with a designer you're happy with, excellent. However, has anyone told you about going the designer-then-builder path versus the design-build path, and why it matters so much?"

Many look puzzled and say, "No, what's that?"

Bethany continues: "Well, the major difference is—actually, you know what? Let me give you an example. See, when Megan came to us . . ." Bethany then wraps it up with: "So, of course, I'm not saying if you design and build separately this will happen to you, and I really hope it doesn't. However, regardless of whether you use us or another design-build option, I strongly suggest you explore the possibility."

When they do, who do you think they'll see as the only logical choice?

Isn't that so much easier than self-promotion or feeling like you're coming across as instilling fear? A simple story neatly sidesteps all that. You're not expressly telling them they're doing it wrong, so it doesn't come across as judgmental. You're not lecturing. You're not even saying they should hire you or that their way won't work for them. For Bethany, her story served as a way to educate prospects on the risks while inspiring interest in a different way of going about the process. It showed that Bethany understood her listeners, their fears, and how to avoid them.

Megan's story and two others catapulted Jenkins Custom Homes from an annual turnover of $6 million after almost twenty years of operation, to more than $18 million the following year.

More important than that, it took an introvert from hating the idea of selling and networking to loving it and dominating her industry! That's the transformative power of story.

WE ALL TELL STORIES

Think about when someone asks how you met your partner. Don't you have a "how we met" story that you've told over and over again? The first time, you probably didn't tell it all that well. But as you got more and more chances to tell it, you told it better and better. You'd notice the parts where people leaned in and seemed really interested, so you played those up. You'd also see when people weren't interested or their eyes glazed over. Perhaps you thought to yourself, *I'll just skip those parts next time.* As the months and years go by, it becomes a bit of a theatrical masterpiece, doesn't it?

We love telling these kinds of stories about our real lives, but when it comes to business, our stories become one-dimensional and matter-of-fact: "The customer wanted this, so I gave it to them." End of story. Why do we do this? Why, when it comes to telling a story to our prospective clients or employers, do we take out all the rich descriptions and emotional context? Why do we take out everything that makes a story engaging and compelling, leaving just the bare-bones facts?

Or, even more common, why does it never occur to us to tell stories at all and instead launch into "teaching mode" whenever the opportunity arises?

I made this exact mistake the first time I spoke from a stage. I still remember when the Economic Development Department of Macedon Ranges Council, in Victoria, Australia, reached out to me. They asked me if I was open to sharing my sales and marketing experience with a group of small-business owners. I was so honored to be asked that I put together the most informative and detailed presentation I could. I shared statistics, strategies, ideologies, scripts, frameworks, processes, and checklists. I gave them everything but the kitchen sink.

I thought I was helping the attendees, but I discovered later that, to them, it felt more like standing in front of a fire hose.

Yes, many attendees told me afterwards that they loved my energy, and that they took pages of notes. They thanked me for being so helpful. But I never heard from any of them ever again.

There's an old sales truism that goes, "Confuse the customer, lose the sale." For me, the devil was in the details. I gave them way too much information and industry jargon. How could they not be overwhelmed after I'd downloaded years of experience in just ninety minutes? Not only had no one contacted me, but very likely no one had applied a single thing I said.

Sure, I'd shown them how smart I was, but I didn't drive any of them to take action, so ultimately, I failed.

Sometimes, when networking, that magical thing happens when you tell someone what you do and they reply, "Oh, I actually need help with that." Do you go right into teaching mode, asking a few questions, then providing advice, solutions, and insights? To you, it feels like you're being helpful and showcasing your expertise. What you're actually doing, however, is just a data dump. The person you do this to may be thankful, knowing you were trying to help—but they'll also be overwhelmed.

Your job when networking is not to download a lifetime of experience but, instead, to tell a powerful story that educates and inspires action. If you do this, listeners will feel a greater connection to you. They'll feel that you're giving them phenomenal value, and they'll be much more likely to want to work with you.

As soon as I started delivering story-rich presentations, far more attendees told me how much value I'd given them. People finally started to come back later, saying that they implemented what I suggested and received amazing results. Better than that, many more reached out to schedule calls to work with me directly. Why? It became more tangible to them. They could see how much my ideas applied to their situation and why they should care. They could also see I really understood their issues and that my strategies could help. This is much better than simply blasting people with a ton of ideas.

In networking, how long do you have to hook someone's attention? Just a few minutes at best, right? You've got to be extremely strategic in those few minutes.

The best vehicle for making them want more is stories.

THE SCIENCE OF STORYTELLING

When I started using stories to network, I could immediately see their power.

Not only did stories allow me to feel more comfortable when sharing the value of what I did, I noticed that it more easily opened up conversation. People could let their guard down and truly listen.

Of course, I knew my niche, and my stories always spoke to them directly—which might partially account for why I'd receive responses like, "I have the exact same problems," or "I need exactly what you did for them!"

But that couldn't be all there was to it.

As I dug into the science, I quickly began to understand. My first discovery was that Princeton neuroscientist Uri Hasson had uncovered evidence of what's known as "neural coupling." When we hear a story, our brains begin to synchronize with the storyteller's. In other words, me telling you a story synchronizes our brain waves! How cool is that?!

This is thanks, in part, to the magic of mirror neurons, discovered by researchers at the University of Parma in the 1980s while studying macaque monkeys. Since then, numerous other researchers have confirmed the phenomenon in both monkeys and humans using fMRIs.

Here's how it works: If you saw me lick ice cream, the same part of your brain fires as if you were eating the ice cream yourself. It's why the crowd collectively gasps when there's an injury on the field. Everyone's mirror neurons, to some degree, make them feel as if the injury had happened to them personally. We can, to an extent, literally feel their pain.

And as Hasson discovered, this happens when we're listening to a story too. If you cringed when someone was telling you about the time they broke their arm, that's your mirror neurons aligning with theirs. It's why we get scared when we're watching a scary movie. Of course we know we're in a movie theater or in our home. Rationally, there's no reason to be scared. But we feel scared nevertheless, because our mirror neurons automatically empathize with the fictional character we see on-screen.

Ultimately, when we hear stories, we can't help feeling as if it's happening to us. It's why Bethany's prospects felt Megan's dismay at her design disaster. Their brains thought they were part of the experience.

This means that by the end of your story, if you've structured and told it well, you and your listener will have gone through a journey together. According to your brains, you now have a shared experience that fosters a real connection.

The next big discovery I made was that story basically short-circuits the logical brain, allowing you to speak directly to the emotional one. This gives you a huge advantage in the net-working room.

See, the logical part of the brain hears facts and details, then thinks, "That won't work for me because . . ." or "Do I really have time for this?" The emotional part of our brain, on the other hand, doesn't analyze any of the logical details. When it hears a story, it just listens. It's almost like the brain excitedly yells out, "Story time!" puts its feet up, and enjoys the show.

To understand why this is the case, we need a quick lesson in how our brains work. The best layman's model I've found is that of the triune brain, which states that we essentially have three areas of our brains:

▶ The neocortex, responsible for our conscious, logical thinking

➤ The limbic system, responsible for our emotions
➤ The "lizard brain," responsible for our basic instincts

We're only really aware of the thinking we do in the neocortex, what we think of as "thinking." But as Nobel-prize winner Daniel Kahneman and many others have demonstrated, most of our decision-making starts with our lizard brain and limbic system—what we call our subconscious. Our lizard brain looks for danger signs, constantly sorting things into friend or foe categories. And our limbic system attaches emotions to what we experience. It's why, after getting food poisoning at a restaurant, the thought of eating there again makes you queasy. That's your limbic system remembering the awful experience it had last time.

In the networking room, as an introvert, you may get caught off guard, leading you to freeze or react in a way you wish you didn't; that's your lizard brain. When you get home, you might get upset or annoyed with yourself for what you said or didn't say; that's your emotional brain kicking in. The next day, you think, "Crap, I should have just said . . ." That's your logical brain finally coming to the party.

When presented with new details and facts, our lizard brain does its job and identifies the source as friend or foe. Anyone we don't really know is abruptly moved into the foe category.

I have no doubt that you've felt the effects of this firsthand. Ever had someone say to you, "Yes, but my situation's different," or "That won't work for me," or "Sounds too good to be true" . . . all before really taking the time to consider what you told them? Or perhaps without even giving you the chance to explain? That's their neocortex swiftly going to work to protect them.

The incredible thing about mirror neurons created through storytelling is that they bypass these mental "gatekeepers." Because the mirror neurons are activated inside our own mind, our logical brain automatically considers the information as coming from a trusted source. That doesn't mean that people always believe a story, but they are much more likely to. Plus, they can't help being captivated by a good one.

(Of course, with great power comes great responsibility: Don't fabricate stories and don't use stories to sell bad products and services. Take the time to find something you really believe in. Then share the amazing outcomes with the world.)

The last discovery I want to share with you is from Stanford professor Jennifer Aaker. She found that people can remember up to twenty-two times more information when embedded into a story than when listed as just plain facts.

Think about what an advantage that is, especially for those offering complex products and services.

When I sold telecommunications, I'd sometimes see a stack of brochures from other salespeople sitting on the prospect's desk. Instead of worrying about the intense competition, I used to get excited. I knew that the prospect would likely remember far more of what I shared with them than from all the other salespeople combined as long as I embedded everything within a story.

Plus, thanks to the power of neural coupling, I also knew that showing what we could do through story, as opposed to telling them what we could do—like everyone else—would create a shared experience, foster a real connection, and increase my chances of a sale.

I understand that the idea of remembering twenty-two times more information—just because it's in a story—might be a little hard to believe. I had trouble believing it myself, despite the success I was having.

Which is why, when I share this information from the stage, I take the attendees through a mental exercise to embrace the truth for themselves.

I'll pick a willing volunteer and tell them, "Okay, I want you to remember three random items, without writing them down: chairs, porridge, beds."

The volunteer usually responds, somewhat uncomfortably, "Okay."

"Now in one year, I'm going to come back to you, and I want you to tell me exactly what those three items are. Oh, and the order I listed them in. What do you think your chances are of remembering?"

They generally laugh and say something like, "Zero to none!"

But when I then ask the audience to recall the story of "Goldilocks and the Three Bears," everyone smiles and nods, understanding my point.

Even though you likely haven't told or heard that story in years, we all know the basics. The little girl sat in some chairs, ate some porridge, slept in some beds.

Now what if I asked you the question again? Do you think you'd have trouble remembering "chairs, porridge, beds" in the right order? Of course not. Because the information is no longer a random list; it's anchored in a story.

You might not remember what you had for dinner last Wednesday night, but you know exactly what time Cinderella's carriage turned into a pumpkin. We remember stories.

USING STORIES IN BUSINESS

When I tell people to use stories, many believe they need to create hundreds. After all, every customer or employer is different, right? This is where having a niche really helps reduce your work: these people have mostly the same problems. Which is why, instead of having lots of stories, I find you can get away with just three—one for each of the main problems, wants, or needs that your niche has.

To craft your three compelling stories, you just need to ask yourself these questions:

1. What are the three major issues, problems, or desired outcomes my niche has/wants? (You identified these in the last chapter.)
2. What is the solution, suggestion, strategy, product, or implementation I recommend to my niche, for each of the three problems or outcomes above?
3. What is one story I have (or that we have as an organization) that describes someone who had one of those problems, issues, or desired outcomes, then implemented my solution and got positive results?

Simple, right?

Now, before I show you how to structure these stories in a way that educates and inspires action, let me provide you with three pieces of advice.

First, don't try to cover all three problems, issues, or desired outcomes in just one story. For instance, I helped Bethany with far more than just storytelling. In fact, that's the case for almost all the people in this book. But when I tell their stories, I don't include all the details, just the parts relevant to the point at hand. So with Bethany, I talk about the main driver in going from $6 million to $18 million within just twelve months—storytelling. While it may be tempting to include more key elements, especially if they all delivered great results or go hand in hand, doing this will overwhelm your prospective customer or employer. Remember, you want to inspire action, not open up the fire hose!

Second, even if you feel like you could create ten amazing stories, I'd still recommend you start with just three. You might be surprised to find you never need another. Even though I now have dozens of stories, I still keep telling the same three when networking. Why? Because they work, and because I've told them hundreds of times. I tell them almost as well as the story of how I met my wife. (Don't let her know, but I may even tell them a little better!)

Third, remember that the story is not about you; it's about the real person you helped. That's where the impact is.

Let me give you an example.

In 2018, I was hired by a multibillion-dollar enterprise to teach their sales force how to effectively use stories. As part of that engagement, we agreed that I would uncover, write, and deliver three stories without notes, to show how easy learning and delivering stories could be.

To find the best stories, I interviewed five groups of salespeople. On one such call, the group told me all about one of their big success stories—migrating a huge government agency to the cloud. Before I ended the call, I retold them the story in about forty-five seconds. One of the group members, amazed with how easily and compellingly I retold the story, asked, "How did you do that?!"

"With a formula," I said (the same formula I'm about to share with you). "However," I went on, "there are two things I'm missing that would make this story so much better. First, the story you told me was about a company and their chief information officer. What was his name?"

"David," one of them replied.

"It's important you use the person's name, not his or her company name or position," I responded. I went on to explain that you can't feel the emotions of a company or a position title, but you can certainly feel the emotions of David going through a major technology transformation. The worry of it all going wrong, the stress of the problems, and the excitement of what a successful implementation could do for his career. We can feel it all.

Moving on to the second missing item, I said to the group, "You'd all been recommending to David that he move to the cloud for years. Why did he decide to move forward now? What changed?"

They didn't know.

It's common for most people not to know all the details for their stories, but that doesn't mean that you should leave those details out. Like Jon Harris, the printer, you need to pick up the phone to find out. In fact, I suggest you do this even if you think you have all the facts. It's often the details that don't even occur to us that become the best part of our stories.

As it turns out, David operated out of an "if it ain't broke, don't fix it" mentality. But then, right before Christmas, their on-site servers crashed, and they couldn't run payroll.

Can you imagine being David, responsible for no one getting paid, going into the biggest spending season of the year? Spending his Christmas holiday worried about losing his job, working day and night to get the systems back up? Feeling guilty for all the stress it caused his team—and their families, who missed them for most of the holidays?

David hated that he was "that guy," the one who ruined Christmas. So, as anyone would, as soon as the holidays were over, he opted to migrate everything to the cloud, drastically reducing the chances of anything ever going wrong again.

See what these extras do for the narrative? Adding in the harrowing details of a server crashing before Christmas, David's whole department having to miss the holidays with their families, employees across the organization not getting gifts, or maybe the landlord knocking at their doors—all this, when connected to how it affected David, turns it into an emotional, three-dimensional story.

Just three stories have propelled my business into rapid growth. It's the same way for most of my clients, even the multimillion-dollar ones. Instead of focusing on crafting more stories, we ensured that each story was perfectly constructed, rich in emotion, and centered on real people. We took the time to really understand the details, considered every element of what went into them, and were disciplined about sharing only one lesson in each. Because of that care, because of the time we took, and because we didn't overcomplicate things, our stories now work almost every time.

So how do you tell a good story? It's really quite simple.

THE STRUCTURE OF A GOOD STORY

A powerful story has four primary parts:

1. **The Problem, Want, or Need:** You want to start by talking about the "before" state of a real person. What was life like before you came on the scene? What were they working toward? What were they excited about? What pain were they experiencing? What problems were they having? Were they worried about losing their job or missing their annual bonus? What kept them up at night? Were there any costs that they weren't even aware of? Describe in detail what was going on in their professional and personal lives. What was their issue costing them, financially and emotionally? Why were their families/bosses/staff/customers upset with them? Highlight those emotions; help your listeners genuinely empathize with their plight, feeling like they're going through the same headaches and heartaches. Spend about 35 percent of your story here.

2. **Analysis and Implementation:** You want to share the epiphany experience, the realization made, and the journey the real person went on. Remember, it's not about you. Do your best to stay away from statements like, "I did this and suggested that," and focus on using more collaborative language, like, "As we implemented stage one together, David was relieved to see just how easy the migration process was." And I cannot emphasize this enough: do not teach. You don't want to

awaken the logical brain. You want your listeners to think "Story time!" and enjoy the show. I suggest you spend a maximum of 20 percent of your time on this section.

3. **Outcome:** The "after" state. This is where you recap the costs saved, trouble avoided, and results obtained. Did they make money or stop losing it? Are they fitter and thinner? Are they happier, less stressed, sleeping better at night? Are they home more with their children? Were there any unexpected benefits? Paint a bright picture, the outcome your listener really wants. Make sure to emphasize the emotional relief or benefits of the after state. Focus about 35 percent of your story on the outcome.

4. **Moral/High-Level Learning:** Never let your listeners draw their own conclusions, because you never know where their minds might go. People telling a story always think the moral is obvious. And it is—for each person, individually. Don't leave it to chance. Instead, spell it out, just as it's done at the end of a fairy tale or one of Aesop's fables. One of my favorite TV shows growing up was *Scrubs*. At the end, JD would always tell you what he learned through the episode's experience. It really brought the core message home for me. Without it, I might have missed the bigger picture altogether. At the end of your story, you want the listener to understand why he or she needs help and to see you as the perfect person to provide it. Nothing brings this home more than a strong and well-articulated moral. Spend the last 10 percent of your story here.

Remember, you want to demonstrate that you completely understand your listener, not just the product or service that you're providing. To do this well, fleshing out the problem, want, or need is critical. I find that most people only touch on the problem, saying something like, "The client didn't have enough customers and wanted more." But there's always much more to it than that. So let's take a moment to broaden your field of vision.

A problem usually has three costs:

1. **Financial Costs:** What did the problem cost them in dollars wasted or lost, additional labor and material, lost customers, missed deadlines, penalties, etc.? What are they losing in real-world dollars and cents?

2. **Opportunity Costs:** This is usually a much bigger number, or of much greater importance. What did it cost them in potential opportunities, like referrals, repeat business, missed customers/projects/contracts? Was it stopping them from losing weight, achieving a goal, getting more responsibility at work, spending more time with their families? In other words, did their big problem prevent them from getting or being offered something else?

3. **Emotional Costs:** What toll is it having on them, their families, their staff, and any other stakeholders? Is the problem causing them stress, worry, anxiety, restlessness? Is the problem causing their families to feel neglected, underappreciated, or sad?

Let me share a story with you, to help you better understand how all of this goes together.

Back in the days I'd just started selling nationally accredited education courses, I booked an appointment with a small-business owner, an electrician named Joe.

While I was excited to have locked down an appointment, Joe's office was in Lilydale. This was about an hour's drive from my office. So an hour out there, thirty- to forty-five minutes for a meeting, an hour back—this trip was going to take up my entire morning.

When I finally arrived and we sat down in his office, I started with one of my standard questions. "Joe, what are the biggest problems you have in your business?"

"I don't really have any problems in my business." I could kind of tell that he was thinking, "Who is this kid trying to tell me I have problems?"

"Really? Because the last sixty electricians I've spoken to over the last thirty days have said they have [this problem, this problem, or this problem]. Are you sure you don't have any of those?"

At this stage, the customer would usually say, "Well . . . actually I have all those problems, too, plus a couple more." That's the benefit of having a niche: you know more about them than they know about themselves. Their guard drops. You go from being a salesperson to a consultant, and they tell you everything.

Instead, Joe said, "Nope, not really."

I remember thinking, "Wow, what am I going to do? I just drove all the way out here. I don't want to waste half my day for nothing!" Out loud, I said, "Well, do you have any problems at all?"

He scratched his chin and said, "Humph. I guess if I had one problem it would be . . . sometimes my staff don't clean up after themselves on the job site."

I jumped on that slim chink in his otherwise impenetrable armor. "So how much is that costing you?"

"Not much. Maybe a half hour of work here and there because I have to send them back to clean up."

So his financial costs were almost nothing. On to opportunity costs.

"Can I ask you a question? Do you still go see customers yourself? To do the work, I mean?"

"Sure, but not as many as my staff. I might see ten people a month. Each of my guys sees four times that."

"Okay," I said, warming up, "do you ever get referrals from the customers you see?"

"All the time. Probably at least three out of those ten."

I got him to talk about the quality of those referrals versus new jobs. As it turns out, phone calls from new customers were often small jobs—maybe someone wanting a ceiling fan installed. The real money came from the referrals, thousands of dollars for bigger jobs, like rewiring an entire factory.

"Wow," I said. "Do your staff get referrals like you?"

"Sometimes, but they'd be lucky to get one or two a month."

Now I could really show him what he was missing, using his own math. "So you're telling me that you see ten people and get at least three referrals, making a minimum of $3,000 from them and sometimes a lot more. Meanwhile, your staff sees four times as many clients as you do but are coming back to the office with maybe two referrals?"

"Yes," he replied, with a puzzled look on his face.

I pressed on. "This worries me. Obviously you can't, but if you were doing those forty jobs a month instead of each of your staff members, you'd be bringing in at least $12,000 in referrals from them, instead of the $2,000 that you're actually getting. So you're losing about $10,000 a month in lost referrals, per staff member. Exactly how many staff do you have?"

Joe began to look concerned, responding, "Five."

"Wow, so you could be losing around $50,000 a month in referrals. Have you ever wondered if the reason your staff aren't getting as many referrals is because they're not cleaning up after themselves? Do you think that your team not having adequate customer service training might be why they don't think cleaning up is important? I wonder what else they're doing wrong that you're not aware of?"

"I never thought of it that way—you might be right!"

So we'd found some big opportunity costs. On to emotional costs.

I then asked, "Joe, does it stress you out knowing your staff could be losing you $50,000 every month all because they don't clean up?"

"Well, it does now!"

I then said, "Now let me ask you this: Is there ever a Friday night when, just before going home, you get a call from an unhappy client about a staff member who didn't clean up, so you have to go do it yourself, missing a kid's dance recital or football game?"

"It happens all the time! Actually, my daughter isn't speaking to me right now because I missed her school play last week. But what can I do? This is what pays the bills. Just one bad Yelp or Google review and we're dead."

Here's something salespeople have known for years: we make decisions emotionally, then use logic to justify them. Once Joe realized how much his problem was costing him at an emotional level, he was sold. He wanted to get started right away. The financial and opportunity costs gave his logical mind a reason to justify his decision.

Later, when I went to networking events, this story became one of my favorites to share. As per the formula, I devoted about 35 percent of my time to explaining how Joe thought he didn't have any problems, then discovering his small real costs, huge opportunity costs, and the heavy emotional toll affecting him and his family. Then, I spent about 20 percent of the time talking about how we provided his team customer service training, how they loved the fast-track format, how much they appreciated our trade-specific educators, and how they really enjoyed their whole experience—making a special note of how uncommon it is for tradespeople to actually enjoy classroom training.

Next, I spent about 35 percent talking about the outcomes.

- Joe saved a few hours of labor a week from not having to send his guys back out to clean up or go out himself.
- The additional surprise of no longer having to advertise because he got more than enough referrals to keep him busy (a big cost savings we discovered only later because he gave us a huge testimonial).
- How within just a few months his staff were averaging about seven or eight referrals per forty visits instead of a

"lucky" one or two, meaning at least an additional $25,000 per month or $300,000 a year (effectively doubling his business).

▶ How much happier he, his wife, and daughter were now that he had more control over his life and time to devote to his family, making a joke out of how they are all speaking to him again.

Then I shared the moral of the story. "So while you think you may not have any problems in your business, it's often the problems you don't even know about that could be costing you hundreds of thousands of dollars. Imagine if Joe had met me a year earlier. He'd have, at minimum, an extra $300,000 in his bank account, not to mention the advertising savings. And he'd have a whole extra year spent with a happier family."

Imagine for a second you were an electrician who thought you didn't have any problems and I told you this story. Wouldn't you want to invite me to your office, or at least to chat over coffee, just to be 100 percent certain you were right?

That's the power of a well-articulated, three-dimensional story.

It's your secret weapon in networking.

our difference defines us

Why fit in when you were born to stand out?

—attributed to DR. SEUSS

Whitney Cole's dream business was fast becoming a nightmare.

After launching as a copywriter and content strategist, things had gone well at first. She'd managed to secure four clients, each paying her a $2,500 retainer. She was doing the work she loved and getting to choose her own hours. Life was looking good.

Unfortunately, after a long period of solid revenue, those four clients abruptly became two within a matter of weeks.

Confronted with the news that her income had been cut in half, Whitney sprang into action. But while motivated to find clients, she was met with the realities of a new and fiercely competitive global marketplace. For the first time, she was not only competing against other local agencies and freelancers but every agency across the world, many of which—likely in the desperate hustle to survive themselves—were willing to cut their prices to the bone. She also found herself having to compete against millions of digital nomads, many enjoying the low cost of living that comes from working from a beach in Thailand or Colombia, willing to work for cents on the dollar.

Whitney felt trapped in a massively commoditized industry, in which people didn't see a benefit in long-term retainers, and in which she felt pressured to price ridiculously low. She was working twice as hard, for a lot less money, and with no real income security.

If that weren't tough enough, in the nine and a half weeks it took to fit her into my schedule, things took a turn for the worse. Yet another client made the decision to no longer outsource work, taking her retainer count to just one. I still remember Whitney saying during our first session together that she was now earning less than what she paid for childcare. If we couldn't fix things and fix them fast, it would be the end of the line for her small business.

Luckily, by that stage, I'd already completed my review of Whitney's business, and I had a plan ready to go. I'd noticed during my review that she seemed to have an affinity for the health technology space. While the connection to health tech wasn't specifically mentioned, I could tell there was something there, buried between the lines of everything she'd provided me. When I asked her about it, she was surprised by my question and said, "I can't believe you noticed. Um, I don't really talk about this much, but . . ." and then explained how, if it weren't for new medical advancements, she likely wouldn't have survived her three open-heart surgeries. As she spoke, I could hear the passion in her voice. Of course she was passionate—health technology had saved her life!

I then said, "Let's explore this passion a little bit. Let me ask you this: Does it frustrate you that companies like Coca-Cola and Red Bull, whose products likely have a negative effect on health, all have enormous marketing budgets and saturate all media channels, making it harder for many life-improving and lifesaving technologies to be heard through the noise?"

"Yes—a lot!"

"Is it also fair to say that you would derive a lot of joy in learning new and targeted marketing strategies, synthesizing them with what you already know, to help mission-focused health technology companies cut through that noise, getting their products in front of those in desperate need?"

"Oh my gosh, yes!"

"Terrific! We have a niche you're passionate about. Now, tell me a little about why they struggle with content marketing and strategy."

"That's easy. They all make the same mistakes." Whitney explained that most health technology companies don't really have their ideal customer in mind when they write new content or share posts on social media. This leads to them sharing things that either focus on impressing their golf buddies (like bragging about obtaining new venture capital funding) or highlighting new features of their products in e-books and white papers (without really explaining the relevance of these features to the potential end user).

"After spending tens of thousands of dollars on e-books, social management, and content marketing, they give up and reallocate that money to paid ads," she said. "This starts a vicious cycle, as the moment they stop spending money on ads, their leads dry up."

I remember being impressed by the level of understanding she had for a market that, until I mentioned it, was just another demographic of clients to her. So I challenged her further: "Whitney, what are three things you could do for these customers to help them fix this?" (This is a variation on the question we explored earlier: What are your niche's three main problems?)

"Simple," she said. "First, I would help them clearly articulate who their avatar is so we know exactly who we're targeting and why they need the products. Second, I would audit their current content to help them realize that there's nothing they're sharing on any of their marketing channels that speaks to their avatar. I would then map out a tree of content ideas that would focus on their avatar directly and that I could write over the coming weeks and months. Third, since content is useless unless it gets in front of their exact right audience, I would create a plan for them to ensure they are sharing the right content on the right channels at the right time."

I responded, "Whitney, that's a fantastic offering. However, if you leave out the long-term writing service—which I know is key to your retainer work, but bear with me—you have the makings of what I call a 'Trojan Horse package.'"

I explained that many prospects find it uncomfortable to commit to recurring retainers (in any industry), especially when it's with someone they just met. And, while this was something we could overcome with a well-structured sales process, we could make the sale even easier by reframing the decision altogether.

The goal of a Trojan Horse package is exactly as it sounds: to get through the door. By not mentioning long-term copywriting services to new prospects, Whitney could get through the door by positioning herself as a trusted and unbiased third-party expert: someone who helps struggling health technology companies uncover why their current marketing and content initiatives are not working.

I explained to Whitney that by doing this, she could charge $3,500 for welcomed advice, and upon hearing her recommendations for creating long-term content, CEOs would likely jump to hire her to write it—skipping the proposal process altogether and securing a retainer without even asking.

Whitney, starting to get excited by the idea, said, "That would be amazing!"

Now Whitney had everything she needed to dominate in the healthcare industry, except for the most critical requirement to success—a way of getting herself out of the commodity box.

I explained to Whitney that regardless of all her great ideas and her passion for the industry, introducing herself as a copywriter or content strategist would put her in the same category they've dismissed many times before.

"You need to define who you are, not your functional skill," I said. "Your skills all by themselves don't speak to your uniqueness, passion, and lifetime of expertise. You need to define yourself in a way that sidesteps the competition altogether—that positions you as a category of one. To achieve this, why don't we call you the Mission Maven?"

I thought the name was a perfect fit for her.

- The word *mission* signified her specialty in helping mission-based health technology companies.
- The word *maven* is defined as "a person who has special knowledge or experience; an expert." It is derived from

the Hebrew word *mebin*, meaning "a person with under-standing, a teacher."

As soon as I shared this with Whitney, she loved it.

"Now, instead of being asked what you do and responding with your functional skills, you can say, 'I am the Mission Maven.' Full stop! It will change the whole balance of a first discussion. They'll be intrigued. They won't be able to stop themselves from asking, 'What's that?' Which is all the invitation you need to explain."

Soon, Whitney was ready to go to market. She knew her niche and was highly passionate to serve it; we'd finalized her stories and sales process; she had a packaging and pricing structure; and she had a name that inspired interest and set her apart.

Within forty-five days of our sessions, Whitney landed her first client as the Mission Maven using the Trojan Horse packaging. On completion of the engagement, Whitney presented the client with her suggested strategies, as well as her full scope-of-work recommendations. As she transitioned into her advice for ensuring that whomever they hired was up to the task, the client interrupted her and said, "Can't you just do it for us?"

She replied as we'd planned: "We do work with a select group of VIP clients to allow us to try new things and stay at the top of our game. I have to say, we've loved working with you and your team, and we really think your product offers a huge benefit to those who need it. So, absolutely, we'd love to work with you on this project. The cost of doing that is $10,000 a month. Does that work for you?"

The client said, "Great, let's do it!"

Think about how much of a flip this is. Whitney went from hard-selling $2,500 monthly retainers to instead being invited in as the Mission Maven to consult in the specialized health tech space. No tendering process. No real "sales" at all.

Within months, she landed multiple clients using this strategy, and grew her recurring revenue to $35,000 a month.

Soon afterward, her business became of interest to a big digital agency. Whitney had met the founder at a networking retreat, and he was impressed by how easily she got in front of impossible-to-access health tech companies. Seeing her uniqueness as the key to her success, he offered to buy her entire company.

Today, the Mission Maven heads up her own department inside a larger agency, works her own hours, and manages her own team of mission mavens as she sees fit. This, just eighteen months after almost giving up on her dream business.

While there were many elements to Whitney's success, calling herself the Mission Maven was the key to garnering interest in a usually impossible marketplace.

That's the power of what I call a Unified Message (UM). It's the magic piece of the puzzle, the catalyst to interest and rapid growth within your target niche. It's just one, two, or three perfect words that will change the trajectory of your business or career forever.

Remember Charlene from chapter 1, and her passion for creating backyard oases? When someone asked what she did, she couldn't exactly launch right into talking about her passion and mission. Can you imagine someone doing that to you? You'd be thinking, "Oh my gosh, I didn't ask for her life purpose—how do I get away from this lady?!" She sure couldn't say, "Oh, I create gorgeous backyard oases for people." As soon as she did, people would ask if she was a landscape architect. Maybe a landscaper? Then she would be right back into defensive mode, explaining that she didn't have the tertiary qualifications or didn't actually do the dirty work.

Instead, she simply introduces herself as the Nature Harmonizer.

A Unified Message is the hook that gets people to lean in. It is the key to starting a networking conversation on the right foot, so you never feel salesy or inauthentic. It works for people just getting started in their businesses and careers. It works for midlevel managers and struggling-to-survive freelancers. It works for multimillion-dollar business founders. It even works for me . . . which is where this idea all began.

They say, "Necessity is the mother of invention." It was absolutely the case for me.

THE MISTAKE THAT CHANGED EVERYTHING

When I first moved to the US, I did exactly what I've just told you not to do: I introduced myself by my functional skill. To this day, I vividly remember the first person who asked me what I did. He was a guy who lived in my apartment complex, who'd just shared with me that he owned a gym. Naturally, as I had just asked him what he did, he gave me the courtesy of asking me the same. Unfortunately, I was anything but ready to answer the question.

See, back home in Melbourne, Australia, I grew up in a working-class family. After getting laid off from my first full-time job just weeks before Christmas and right out of high school, the only job that I could get was in door-to-door sales—terrifying for all of us introverts, right? Well, after ninety-two doors of rejection just in my first day, I started teaching myself how to sell watching YouTube videos at night. After six grueling weeks of practice and real-world selling, my manager called me into his office to tell me I was the number one performer in the company. So naturally he promoted me and gave me my very own team of twenty salespeople. My sales team began to excel, and I was promoted a further six more times inside a year. Finally, I decided to go into business for myself. In less than a year, we'd made more than $1 million. Fast-forward a decade and I'd been responsible for five multi-million-dollar success stories. And now, I was dedicated to taking everything I'd learned into my newfound passion for helping small-business owners.

How could I possibly communicate all that in just a few seconds?

I could have said, "Oh, it's complicated." But that's true for everyone reading this book. We all have a lifetime of unique experiences, victories, insights, learnings, and outlooks. We are all so many things, but in truth . . . nobody cares. Or, at least, not enough to endure a detailed explanation after a simple question. So then, how could I simplify it and still communicate my experience and credibility?

I decided to go with the most straightforward, uncomplicated answer I had.

I simply told him, "Oh, I'm a sales coach."

He immediately went cold. He started talking about the sales coach he'd hired a few years ago who sounded like he was one notch above a scam artist. At this point, he was now looking at me like I was one notch above a scam artist.

This happens to so many people when they identify as their functional skill. The listener had a bad experience, and so you get lumped into the same "bad guy" category.

"Well, really, mate, I'm not just a sales trainer . . ." I stammered, trying to find my way out of the hole. I tried to tell him about the marketing work I'd done and how I believed that sales had to be part of a broader, overarching strategy. But I'd already lost him. Worse, my feeble attempt to defend what I did made me sound like I was trying to pitch him. After that, even friendship was off the table.

I wasn't trying to be salesy in any way. I'd just moved to a completely new country and wanted to foster a relationship with someone, and he seemed like a nice guy. I'd left a great group of friends back home, and here I knew no one. He asked what I did and I answered him. His brain made the connection, assumed I was going to try to sell him something, lumped me into the "bad guy" box, and cut off any further discussion. This guy lived just a few doors down from me, and now I'd have to walk past him every few days. Awkward, to say the least.

I did not want to go through that again. It hurt. Unlike cold-calling, where I could just shake it off and go to the next door, I found myself replaying it in my head for days. To me, this rejection felt personal, as if it was a rejection of me as a human being. I kept criticizing myself, asking, "Matthew, why did you talk about work at all!"

Turns out, that conversation may have been my lucky break, as my constant analysis of it pushed me to a solution.

The next time somebody asked me that question, I was ready: "I'm a cross between a sales trainer and a marketing coach for small-business owners."

The other person went, "Oh, that's nice." Then stopped. She thought she knew what I did, had no need for it, and that was the end of the discussion. In an effort to keep the dialogue going, I pulled out one of the sales questions I used to ask: "So . . . what issues are you having in your business?" In retrospect, of course, this didn't have a chance of working. I mean, I'd barely said hello and then I was trying to turn the discussion into a sales meeting. She was at a networking event to make connections, not to be sold to. For me, pitching people in a networking space felt lower than cold-calling a sandwich shop at lunchtime—misguided and unappreciated, to say the least. I immediately felt salesy and uncomfortable.

Still not knowing how to resolve the situation, I introduced myself the same way the next time someone asked what I did. This time, his response was, "Oh, I'm looking for a marketing guy—how much do you cost?"

But this was problematic too. I knew from my time in sales that I should never answer this question before understanding the full requirements, and a networking chat was not the time or place for that. He just wanted my hourly rate . . . a price he could use to see if I was in the ballpark compared to all the other marketers he'd likely already spoken to. I was stuck between annoying him with a detailed and unwelcome sales discussion or spitting out a price that was likely going to lose me the gig anyway. Neither were great options.

The next time someone asked me: "Oh, I had a marketing coach once," she answered. "Didn't really help us get new customers."

Well, that was awkward. And painful. I wanted to say, "But wait, I'm better! I'm different! I have magic ruby slippers!" But she didn't care.

I knew I was more than "just" a sales trainer, more than "just" a marketing coach. Once I began talking, I could explain things, but I noticed that as soon as I answered with my functional skills, people put me in a box. After that, like a crab in a bucket, it was nearly impossible to get out.

No doubt the same thing happens to you. "I'm a programmer." "I'm a realtor." "I'm an HR professional." "I'm in customer support." "I work in a call center." The moment you identify yourself this way, the other person puts you in a commodity box.

A commodity is understood to be a material or product that looks pretty much like all its competitors. Milk, for example, is pretty much milk. Rice is rice. Even complex products like TVs are more or less commodities these days. There's no substantial difference between them, so many of us feel it doesn't really matter which one we choose.

You can't blame the people you're networking with, though. It's not their fault. This is how our brains naturally work. We go through the world understanding things by linking them to what we already know.

When the Spanish conquistadors landed in Central America, the indigenous people had never seen horses before; they didn't exist in either North or South America, so they described them as "big dogs." We create these types of linkages, even when they don't really make sense, because our brains are constantly trying to process the world around us. Our brains like to categorize things into neat, easy-to-understand boxes.

To me, it didn't make sense for people to put me in the same box as other sales trainers, as my views on sales and the value I provided were unique. How could someone else possibly have my lifetime of skills and experiences? Ask yourself, given your unique history and achievements, how could any commodity box possibly do you justice? I was different—and so are you. But if you don't communicate that right at the start, the listener's brain will find a box and automatically put you in it . . . even if you don't belong there. And you know the thing about first impressions: once formed, they are tremendously hard to change.

I knew that if I wanted to get out of the box, I needed to start thinking outside it. I needed a way of responding to the question "What do you do?" in a way that would:

- Sidestep my competition
- Communicate the outcome or value I could provide them
- Allude to my passion and mission
- Not pigeonhole myself into something too specific, that wouldn't allow me to grow and change

In other words, I needed one phrase that unified everything in a simple message. Not a slogan, not a tagline, but something that defined who I was, almost on a spiritual level. That's when it came to me: "Why don't I call myself the Rapid Growth® Guy?"

GET INVITED TO SHARE

So how did I drop my Unified Message naturally into a conversation?

When I introduce myself, I'm almost always the first to ask what they do. As an introvert, one of my natural gifts is intently listening and engaging with what a person has to say. I empathize with their response, showing genuine interest and care, and then ask further questions that invite them to go deeper. As I'm speaking to them, something invariably comes up that allows me to offer insight, a suggestion, advice, guidance, or just plain excitement.

Without even realizing it, they are deep into speaking about themselves, which is a pleasant change of pace from all the awkward responses and stilted discussions that networking normally involves.

By providing as much value as I can, and showing a genuine interest in them, the human instinct of reciprocity (read *Influence* by psychologist Robert Cialdini) drives them to afford me the same courtesy. Eventually, our discussion about them comes to an end, or they realize how one-sided our conversation has been, and they say, "Oh my gosh, I never even asked: What is it *you* do?"

I always reply, "I'm the Rapid Growth Guy." I don't rush on ahead into my passion and mission. I don't launch right into a story. In fact, I don't offer any explanation at all. Instead, I state it just as if I were saying, "I'm a sales trainer." I act as if they should know what it means.

Instantly, they transform from having their guard up, preparing for a pitch, and being afraid of me selling them something, to being open, curious, and interested. They can't help asking, "What exactly is that?"

As an introvert, nothing could be better. My whole body chemistry changes when I'm invited to share what I do with somebody, instead of feeling like I have to pitch them. My muscles relax. My breathing slows. And since I'm the only Rapid Growth Guy they've ever met, I don't get stuck in any conversations where the prospect has preconceived thoughts about me or the fees that I can charge.

A Unified Message is the clean slate you need to attract your ideal prospects or employers. Think of it as a slingshot right into a discussion of who you are and the value you can provide.

It's your ticket to leaving your competition in the dust and finally getting paid what you're worth.

THE FEAR OF STANDING OUT

As an introvert, after reading about the idea of creating a Unified Message, you might be thinking to yourself, "I'm just not like that. I'm not comfortable standing out in that way. I don't think a Unified Message is for me."

I get it. It's scary to put yourself out there, not just because you're an introvert, but because as human beings we're all conditioned to play it safe. A few thousand years ago, we all lived in tribes. Being a troublemaker or rabble-rouser might mean being expelled by the chief, which would mean death. Striking off on our own also usually meant death. We learned to conform to the ways of the tribe and not to make waves. So it makes sense that we get uncomfortable at the idea of being different.

But you have to ask yourself: Did the people at the top of an organization or an industry get there by being just like everyone else? Or did they get there by being outliers, being different, being more than just another [fill in the blank]?

This is why I challenge you to leave the constraints of your functional skill behind and decide to be the you you were always destined to be. To not just wait to be noticed but to make people notice by singing your difference from the rooftops. That's what your UM will do for you.

Naomi Stephan wrote, "You have a calling which exists only for you and which only you can fulfill." Why let complete strangers put you in a preconceived box? Why not create your own box with your own label? Why not have a message that perfectly defines your uniqueness and how you help the world? Why not allow yourself to transcend from one of the many to a category of just one?

After all, being the Mission Maven allowed Whitney to rapidly grow her business and even get acquired by a larger agency. It was Justin McCullough's willingness to be different that secured him his high-paying executive role at FSG.

To Justin, Whitney, and so many of my former clients and online students, a Unified Message is a hook, but it's also much more. It doesn't feel like a gimmick. To them, it perfectly defines who they are and the value that they provide.

It takes a lot of courage to step out from the shadows of your functional skill. But it's necessary if you want people to stop treating—and paying—you like you're "just another [enter your functional skill here]."

CRAFTING YOUR OWN UNIFIED MESSAGE

How do you come up with your own Unified Message?

Go back and look at your answers to the last section of chapter 3. Not just the three main problems you solve or outcomes you provide, but all the wonderful things you identified as standout qualities. Looking at all these things that you do, and that your niche really appreciates, ask yourself, "What is the higher-level benefit of all that? What is it that my target niche really gets out of working with me? How can I summarize all of this in just two or three words?"

Wendy is a great example. You might recall that we identified her niche to be high-level executives being relocated to China. The guidance she provided—helping the family as a whole to thrive in a country with far different cultural norms—was her real secret sauce. That's why I suggested we call her the China Success Coach.

It was this message as well as her package, the China Success Intensive, that took her from struggling to make just $50–80 an hour in a saturated market, to making $30,000 per family, with virtually no competition.

Keep in mind, you're not creating a tagline or slogan. Whatever you come up with, you must be able to use it in a sentence: "I am the [UM]." Just like saying, "I'm an accountant."

Here are some other real-life examples:

▶ I help thought leaders and influencers uncover why their website content isn't getting great rankings on Google: the Authority Detective.

- ▶ I work with event planners wanting to create a memorable moment for attendees by providing laser light shows that dance to music: the Memory Weaver.
- ▶ I help traditionally high-achieving executives get out of an uncommon funk: the Plateau Hacker.
- ▶ I work with off-site educators to ensure that their workbooks are correct and arrive on time: the Workbook Concierge.
- ▶ We help businesses with a growth-through-acquisition strategy not to fall victim to complex technology challenges that can kill productivity and cause data vulnerabilities: the Acquisition Lifeguard.
- ▶ More examples, resources, and video interviews with real students can be found in the bonus materials. (See page 231 for more details.)

(Important note: Consider speaking to an attorney before deciding on your UM. I've been told that some words may not be used in specific countries, unless you hold a particular qualification.)

If you get stuck coming up with your UM, that's okay. Don't be afraid to walk away and come back to it multiple times. It may even come to you in the shower or while going for your morning run.

I also recommend you turn to your thesaurus, even if it's just to get you started. Take Alex Murphy, for example. For those who've read my first book, you'll recall that Alex was a struggling videographer who was making almost no money at all, and that through our work together, he was able to grow his business to nearly seven figures in less than a year. Did you ever wonder where the leads for that growth came from? All of them were from networking as the Narrative Strategist!

So how did I come up with his name?

I thought to myself, "Alex wants to tell an organization's story across multiple cohesive videos rather than stand-alone, disjointed ones. What can I do with that?"

To get started, I typed *story* into my laptop's thesaurus. And there it was: the word *narrative*. As soon as I saw it, I thought, "That's perfect. I'll call Alex the Narrative Strategist."

This is a simple example that took me only a few minutes. Most, however, take hours.

Embrace the fact that crafting your UM is a creative process, and just like any creative process, it can get a little messy. Remind yourself that there are no bad ideas and start throwing anything that comes to mind on a page. It's worth the time, the mess, and perhaps a little discomfort to get to that perfect one. After all, you'll get to enjoy the benefits of your hard work every time you go networking—smiling each time you hear people ask, "What exactly is that?"

In creating your UM, ignore the urge to be descriptive; the goal is actually to be somewhat vague and ambiguous. It's designed to be a hook, remember? So many people try to bring their functional skill into it, like calling themselves the Real Estate Diva or the Data Doctor. But these don't get people to ask, "What's that?" If your UM is obvious, they don't need to know more. They have a commodity box that they plunk you right into; the same box that they've dismissed many times before. Think of your UM as a movie trailer. It's not the whole show—it's just the teaser that gets people to buy a ticket to the full movie.

Finally—and this may be the toughest for those with a fear of standing out—I want you to be prepared for the fact that your family and friends will likely disapprove of any UM you come up with, no matter how intriguing it is. They may even think your UM sounds a little silly. This is totally normal, and it's by no means a reflection on your UM. Let me explain.

IGNORE THE ONES YOU LOVE

When I first met Shane Melanson, he told me he was in real estate syndication. Sounds dodgy, right? But while the term may set off an alarm, it's actually the standard name for the type of commercial real estate investing he did. Syndication is basically the name for a pool of investors going in on a project together that, otherwise, would cost too much money or provide too much risk individually.

As we worked through the process of uncovering Shane's niche, I noticed that he'd obtained some really great results for a few doctors and surgeons. As it turned out, his father-in-law was a surgeon and had referred a few of his friends to Shane.

I asked him, "So what's their problem? What keeps them up at night?"

With these high-earning individuals, it's hard to imagine them having any problems, right? I mean, they live the life that many dream of, with big houses, expensive cars, their kids going to all the right schools. But somewhere in their fifties, they start getting worried about retirement. In a way, these professionals are trapped in a pair of golden handcuffs: they can't stop working. The moment they do, their income goes to zero. If their retirement savings aren't enough to let them continue their lifestyle, that's a problem for them. One that keeps them up at night wondering what to do about it.

They hear that residential real estate investing is the way to go. But instead of spending months looking for the exact right purchase, their long and exhausting hours at the hospital or clinic tend to drive them toward snap decision-making.

This often leads to them paying too much for property and, while they may have hired a property manager, dealing with the stress of bad tenants who are late on rent or leave their investment in disrepair. It's not long before they feel burned by the whole experience, as they've often lost money—and, more important to them, time.

Shane was a lifeline to these kinds of people. His whole business focused on showing high-income earners that, while they had expensive lifestyles, their ability to borrow substantial amounts afforded them an opportunity unavailable to others. They could team up with a small group of high-income investors and take advantage of run-down or undervalued commercial properties. Within just a few years, they could turn their investment into real wealth and enjoy the retirement they were hoping for.

Shane's problem, however, was that any time he tried to explain this, he felt like he came across as a commercial real estate salesperson. He also worried that the concept of syndication, to them, came off sounding like a scam.

I said to Shane, "Let's not use the words *commercial real estate* or *syndication* at all. Why not instead call yourself the Arbitrage Architect?"

I explained why I thought the name was a perfect fit:

- ▶ The word *arbitrage* basically means buying low and selling high, making money from the difference. I felt this perfectly described the way Shane helps a pool of investors to purchase, develop, and later sell or rent a commercial property at a premium price.
- ▶ I felt the word *architect* described how he organized deals for investors and oversaw their execution.

Shane loved the name, and he loved the idea of helping doctors transition their income into high net worth and a secure retirement. Our session couldn't have ended on a more positive note.

Before our next meeting, however, he shared his UM with his wife and father-in-law, and unfortunately, it did not go well. Shane told me, "They both looked at me like I was crazy."

His father-in-law said something like, "What are you doing? You're not the Arbitrage Architect, you're in real estate syndication. What's wrong with just saying that?"

Understandably, Shane was rather beaten up about the whole experience. After empathizing with his angst, I explained that their responses were totally normal.

First—and this is the biggest factor—the people who truly care about you want to protect you. They worry about you trying new things. After all, new things might fail, and they'd hate to see you embarrassed. Naturally, they like seeing you play it safe.

Second, many people who do not understand the value of a UM can't imagine calling themselves anything but their functional skill. This was especially true for Shane's surgeon father-in-law, who discouraged him just as he would any doctor friends who decided to call themselves anything other than a doctor.

Third, the only reason Shane's wife and father-in-law had an issue with his UM is because they already knew his functional skill. To them, it was like he'd walked up and said, "My name is no longer Shane. Please call me Tom from now on." What would you think if a loved one or even an acquaintance said this to you? You'd probably think it was strange. But, what if Shane walked up to you at a networking event and said, "Hi, I'm Tom." How would you know any different? To you, his name is Tom.

I still remember making this same mistake myself when I came up with my own UM. In a discussion with an old colleague of mine, completely off the cuff, I said, "I'm going to start calling myself the Rapid Growth Guy. What do you think about that?"

He laughed and said it sounded like a commercial for . . . well, a specific kind of male supplement. Then he proceeded to explain to me that I was a great sales trainer but seemed to have lost my way.

Today, so many people want to be the Rapid Growth Guy that I've had to trademark it.

After explaining all this, I said, "Shane, I know it's hard, but I wouldn't put too much weight on what your wife and father-in-law think. Remember, a UM is a hook to get new prospects excited and inspired to want to know more about you. That's it! To them, you're the Arbitrage Architect, and because they've never heard of that before, they'll be interested to learn more."

Shane, emboldened by our discussion, took his powerful message to the networking room. And it worked!

Today, almost a year after agreeing to have faith in his UM, Shane's business has exploded.

- ▶ He's been able to raise more than $1 million in additional capital.
- ▶ In the past he'd have to work hard to discover deals; now the best opportunities reach out to him directly, giving him the luxury of being able to pick and choose.
- ▶ He's in the process of formalizing a partnership with a group of three thousand doctors who reached out to him.
- ▶ He's successfully launched a six-figure coaching business, teaching his investment strategies to high-income doctors.

My advice: When you first come up with your own UM, don't share it with family and friends. Share it with prospects or potential employers, because it's their reactions that really count.

All that matters is, when you're talking to someone in your niche, your UM makes them ask, "What exactly is that?"

The entire goal of a UM is to get invited to share more.

Now, let's talk about the different opportunities your UM presents in the networking room, and how to handle each one.

speak to the right people

The question is not what you look at,
but what you see.

—HENRY DAVID THOREAU

Think about some of the movies you've seen, the ones with the greatest plot twists. There you were, thinking you know what's about to happen, when *bam*!—a big reveal completely changed everything. Whether it was the original *Planet of the Apes*, where you saw the Statue of Liberty and realized they're on a future war-stricken Earth; *Star Wars: The Empire Strikes Back*, when you learned that Darth Vader is Luke's father; or *The Sixth Sense*, when you discovered Bruce Willis's character was a ghost the whole time—whatever movies came to mind, I have no doubt that your jaw dropped a little during the big reveal.

Well, I actually have a plot twist of my own to share.

For the last five chapters, you've read or listened along under the assumption that this book was about networking with new prospects—potential clients or employers—as an introvert.

But, what if I told you that networking is *not* primarily about finding people who want to hire you?

Yes, prospects are your bread and butter. Yes, prospects turn into sales or jobs. But focusing on them and only them is what's keeping you stuck in the hamster wheel.

Here's the plot twist: Networking is really about meeting the people who, after one good networking conversation, could pave the way to a multitude of sales opportunities, the people who could help you land a job far beyond what you'd ever hoped for.

So who are these magical people?

I like to call them *champions* and *momentum partners*.

Champions are an elite group. They're the high achievers and influencers who really make the world go 'round. The people who can seriously give your rocket ship a huge boost. They might be connected with those impossible-to-access individuals. They might have won prestigious awards. Their work might have afforded them a great deal of respect or name recognition. They might have a popular magazine, mailing list, podcast, or social profile. They may hold a high-level leadership position in an association or organization. Whatever the case, champions can lend serious credibility to your mission, as well as open doors for you that are normally locked shut. These people should be your most guarded and cherished network contacts. They should be the individuals you almost never ask anything of. They'll also likely be the people that offer you more support than you could ever expect.

Momentum partners are a small group of connections who willingly open up their Rolodex to you, and for whom you do the same. Whether it's an introduction to a podcast host, a magazine editor, an event organizer, a possible champion, a new prospect, or even another momentum partner, a good partnership should bring a wave of warm connections into the in-boxes of all parties involved. I like to think of these people as being on my rowing team. With all of us pulling together, we reach our destinations much faster.

Take a second to think about your current network. Perhaps even scroll through your connections on LinkedIn. It's likely that you already have many possible momentum partners and champions within your Rolodex. It might be that "big deal" family friend. An old buddy who now has a podcast. A colleague who's just been asked to be on an advisory board.

Of course, if you know no one at all, that's okay too. Remember, when I first moved to Austin, I didn't know a soul. The strategies in this book will lead you, like they did me, to rapid networking success regardless.

But first . . . let me talk to you about a cat in a box.

YOU NEVER KNOW WHO YOU'RE GOING TO MEET

I think of every person I meet in the context of Schrödinger's cat, the thought experiment where you assume something both is and isn't. Erwin Schrödinger, the Austrian physicist who came up with the idea, proposed a scenario wherein a cat would be put in a box with a radioactive atom, a Geiger counter, and a flask of poison. When the atom decayed, the Geiger counter would detect it and go off, shattering the flask and killing the cat. But when would the flask shatter? To someone looking at the closed box, you'd have to assume that the cat was both dead *and* alive. (Disclaimer: no cats were harmed in the making of this thought experiment.)

Or perhaps you find it easier to think of people like Forrest Gump: "My momma always said life was like a box of chocolates: you never know what you're gonna get." That's especially true these days where tech multimillionaires spend a fortune to look like they don't care. Steve Jobs was famous for his turtleneck and jeans. Zuckerberg goes around in a hoodie. One of the owners of the company where I had my first sales job always looked like he'd just come from a Metallica concert, especially with his crazy long hair. You can't judge a book by its cover . . . or a cat by its box.

That's how I approach networking. I treat every person like he or she has the potential to be a prospect, momentum partner, or champion. Every person has the potential to help me on my mission. It's my job to discover how.

I'm going to tell you a couple of "cat in the box" stories that, at first, might seem unbelievably lucky. But just like Louis Pasteur, who said, "Chance favors the prepared mind," I believe in creating my own luck.

Between high school and college, most Australians live it up and party hard. This goes well into their first year of university (much like Americans do, I've heard). Unfortunately, due to my reading issues and my hustle playing catch-up with the rest of my class, I got to the end of high school exhausted. I finished in the top 20 percent of my state, but I had absolutely no idea what I wanted to do with my life. My family and I agreed that I'd never survive university if I didn't know exactly what I wanted out of it. We decided I should take a gap year to really "find myself."

I don't know what you've heard about other people's gap years, but I came from a family that struggled to be even middle class. They certainly couldn't afford to send me traveling all over Europe. Instead, I went right to work.

Just over a year later, I was running my own million-dollar business, and things just got busier from there. There was no partying and lounging around for me.

So, after all my hard-won business success, I decided to finally take a real "gap year" just before my twenty-ninth birthday. I now jokingly call it my "mid-midlife crisis." My good friend Dmitry, when he found out what I had planned, asked if he could join me. We ran with the bulls in Spain and drove through the Swiss Alps. We even went to Carnaval en Salvador (where the real Brazilian carnival happens).

Among our other adventures, we went to South by Southwest in Austin. When we heard there was a big American spring break happening down on the Texas coast, we decided to go see what it was all about. We wanted to see for ourselves if the hype was really true.

We found ourselves on South Padre Island, a world-renowned spring break hotspot. Unfortunately, our first day, Dmitry came down with a nasty bug and was confined to his room. Also on our first day, I had a realization: Here I was, almost in my thirties, and the average age there was probably nineteen. "Man, I'm way too old to be here!" I thought. I didn't know what to do. I didn't want to stay in the room (especially with the way Dmitry looked), but I didn't want to be the sad old dude wandering around either. I walked downstairs to the hotel bar to work out what to do.

I sat down and noticed another guy a little older than me drinking at the bar too. He looked stressed. I thought to myself, "Maybe he's also thinking he made a big mistake coming here." As an introvert, it's not in my nature to start chatting to random strangers, but for years I'd pushed myself to get out of my comfort zone. (I now feel like I'm letting myself down if I don't try out one or two of my conversation starters.)

I finally said, "You okay, mate? You look a bit concerned."

"Yeah, just staff nightmares at work." Naturally, I empathized and shared that, after leading teams myself, I know how stressful that can be.

Then I said, "Anything specific that drove you to that Long Island Iced Tea?"

He started sharing some of his business struggles. I listened and offered some suggestions about what I found had worked for me. After forty-five minutes of great discussion, he asked me what my plans were for the night. I explained that I had intended to go out and experience this spring break thing with my mate, but he was sick in the room and I didn't want to be the old man out on his own.

"Think I'm just going to grab a bite and then pop off to bed. What about you?"

"Oh, I've got to make sure everything keeps running," he said as he gestured around.

"Wait, this is your bar?" I asked, confused.

"No, but this is my event. My company runs a big part of South Padre's and Cancun's spring breaks. And right now I have to head to another club event. I'm with you—too old for all these kids. But there's a VIP section I have where I'm gonna be entertaining some of the folks from MTV and the cast from *The Real World*," he said, referring to a hot reality TV show (though I had no idea what that was at the time). "Want to come along as my guest?"

I went out with him that first night. The next day, Dmitry rallied, and we spent the rest of spring break as the VIP guests of the guy who ran everything. We met Hollywood actors, musicians, and celebrities other people would kill to get an introduction to. Sadly, I'm the guy who knows none of the "big deal" people, so it was a little wasted on me. That said, it meant I treated them just like any other person (which may have been why they seemed to like chatting with me).

After a few nights, though, things started to feel a little monotonous. We'd seen spring break for ourselves and were ready to move on to our next adventure. But I kept in contact with my newfound friend. In fact, his support was a big factor in getting my extraordinary talent visa to the United States the following year.

Luck, right?

Let me ask you this: How many times have you sat down next to someone and made zero effort to engage? How many awesome opportunities have been right next to you on a plane, in a restaurant, or at a bar? Who knows—you might have been sitting next to the very person you've been trying to reach! I should know, as I secured a client on a flight out of my home city airport, Raleigh/Durham International. All I did was ask my seatmate, "So, are you heading home or away for work? . . . Very cool, what's the trip for? Oh, what do I do? I'm the Rapid Growth Guy."

Turns out my seatmate was Stacie McEntyre, the founder and CEO of Veritas Collaborative, one of the largest hospitals in the country for eating disorder treatments. She was experiencing some growing pains in her business and was looking for a way to maintain their culture, aid staff and client on-boarding, increase retention, and drive up productivity—all things a few company-wide stories are great at facilitating.

You might think, "Sure, Matthew, that stuff happens up in business class. I'm usually stuck flying coach." Well, it happens in economy, too, because that's where we were. Part of our initial discussion led to another thing I say often: "So you think business class for domestic flights is a waste of money, too, then?" It always leads them to saying, absolutely, that they'd personally prefer to spend that money on something else. But Stacie's frugality certainly didn't stand in the way of her spending tens of thousands of dollars working with me over the coming months.

These Schrödinger's cats are literally sitting right beside you.

The same thing happened with an Oracle executive during a delay at an airport. We were sitting next to each other at the same restaurant, and I overheard her speaking to a colleague about the delay. I said, "You're delayed, too, are you? Going to be late for anything important?" Our discussion led to us discovering that we were going to the same city, and two of her bosses changed their plans, on short notice, to come and meet me while I was in town.

And these Schrödinger's cats are not just happening in the real world; they are happening online too. A random Face-book post, where I prompted further conversation, turned into getting introduced to a translator, who happened to have a relationship with one of Vietnam's biggest publishers. The result: my first book was translated and published in Vietnamese.

Once something starts occurring regularly, you can't say it's just luck. It's a system—the same system I'm showing you here.

You never know what's in the box unless you open it. Some of your best prospects, momentum partners, and champions are likely walking right by you—or sitting right next to you—without you ever taking advantage of the potential networking opportunity. They may not be dressed like how you'd imagine a champion, momentum partner, or even prospect would be dressed. They may not seem the "right" age. They may not even look like they're open to a discussion. But don't assume the conversation is dead before you open the box. Instead, have the Schrödinger's cat mentality and be open to connecting with people . . . anywhere . . . anytime.

AVOIDING TUNNEL VISION

Strategic networking goes far beyond any networking room: it's a way of life.

Unfortunately for many, however, overcoming what I call "prospect tunnel vision" doesn't come without its challenges.

A time will come when you will meet someone at an event, on a plane, or because they reached out to you for help, and you'll think, "I don't need to open the box—this person is clearly a prospect." Here's why thinking of them through the lens of "prospect tunnel vision" is a mistake.

About five months after moving to the United States, I was lucky enough to get an opportunity to contribute to *Entrepreneur* magazine, thanks to the help of a strong momentum partner. Not long after my first article was published, my phone rang with a number I didn't recognize.

"Hello, this is Matthew."

On the other end of the phone was none other than Judy Robinett. I have to admit, at the time, I didn't know who she was, but it didn't take long for me to realize that she was a big deal.

She shared with me that her first book, *How to Be a Power Connector*—later named by *Inc.* as the number one business book of 2014—had just been published by McGraw-Hill and, due to its success, she was getting quite a few speaking requests. Her problem was that they rarely actually booked her.

Judy had clearly picked up the phone for me to help her with her problem. There was also no doubt that, at the time, her becoming a client would have provided some much-needed credibility and revenue to my relatively new business.

Ask yourself, what would you have done in this situation?

I had to make a decision: Treat Judy like a prospect and put my tried and tested sales process to work? Or explore the possibility of a more long-term, higher-value relationship? It was a tough choice, one I had to make uncomfortably on the fly. But I've been benefiting from that choice ever since.

Understanding that a relationship with someone like Judy could be far more valuable than any short-term financial gain, I decided to explore the possibility of pursuing a relationship with her as a champion or momentum partner.

After a detailed discussion, I saw that she was really only one small tactic away from securing a lot more speaking deals. So I simply shared that tactic as friendly advice.

Instead of trying to sell to her, my willingness to provide that one transformative tactic, asking for nothing in return, led to her becoming a lifelong, enthusiastic momentum partner.

Within days of our conversation, I began to receive warm introductions to podcast hosts, editors of high-traffic blogs, and high-level influencers like Gerhard Gschwandtner, who champions my work in the sales community to this day. In addition to Gerhard providing me with introductions to sales legends like Brian Tracy and Jim Cathcart, when my first book was released, he published a glowing editorial in *Selling Power* magazine and referenced it on the issue's cover.

Seeing that Judy was still in the throes of promoting her new book, I saw the most valuable thing I could do in return was reciprocate with introductions of my own. Naturally, I didn't have anywhere near the connections Judy did. But anyone I met who I thought could offer her value, swiftly got an introduction. I even dropped her name whenever I could in articles I published, interviews I obtained, and elsewhere (as I'm doing right now).

Certainly, as time progressed and my network grew, so did the quality of my introductions. For instance, when the time came for Judy to launch her second book, my network included Jaime Masters, fellow introvert and host of *The Eventual Millionaire* (which *Inc.* and *Entrepreneur* both call one of the best podcasts in the world for entrepreneurs). Turns out that it was one of the easiest introductions to make, as Jaime had been a big fan of Judy's for some time. They're good friends now and caught up when Judy was in Austin.

Today, because I didn't fall victim to prospect tunnel vision, I now have one of the most connected people on Earth as a good friend and advocate. In fact, if you're familiar with my first book, you might recognize her name from the glowing foreword she wrote. You might also remember her calling me "the best friend I've never met." That's how close we've become.

While we've never managed to meet face-to-face, for more than six years we've enjoyed the spoils of a phenomenal partnership—one that I can directly attribute at least forty podcast interviews and well over six figures in revenue to.

She believes in the work I do, just as I believe in hers. While we might be on different missions, we see massive value in helping each other. You might think of us as business partners, each feeding into the other's momentum, mission, and efforts. We're constantly saying, "Tell me what's been going on. . . . Wow, that sounds fantastic! You know who you need to speak to?"

All this because I was willing to broaden my focus and see Judy's phone call as more than just a chance at a single transaction. Instead, I made a conscious decision to sacrifice a little short-term gain.

Sadly, most people's scarcity mind-set, fear of being taken advantage of, shortsightedness, or even selfishness (however unconscious) results in missing out on rewarding relationships like this.

I'm reminded of a time I went to a local speakers' group. The topic was on how to get more speaking gigs. At one point, I stood up and said, "Guys, let me ask you this: After you speak, it's two or three years before they'll invite you back, right?"

Everyone agreed. Organizers like to keep it interesting, so they rotate out, always on the hunt for new ideas and new speakers.

"Well, after you speak, don't you know best what they're looking for and who'd be a great fit for them? Why not recommend someone from this room? It's what I do. After I'm finished speaking, I say, 'You know who I'd recommend as an awesome speaker for you next year?' Then I suggest someone I think would provide phenomenal value to their audience or organization."

I was actually quite shocked at just how quickly the room went quiet. No one seemed to like the idea. What a shame! Can you imagine the deals and referrals the group could have helped one another get? I learned later that many were worried about giving leads and not getting any in return. There was even one person who told me, "I don't want to give up my customers to the competition!" I remember thinking, "This is an industry that spends hundreds of billions in the US alone. Seriously, get out of scarcity mode, mate!"

Scarcity is not the mentality I have, nor one I want to foster. To me, the logic of that local speakers' group didn't make sense at all. I'm forever recommending my champions and momentum partners for paid stage opportunities. After all, I'd rather recommend someone who, in a year or two, might remind them about me. Plus, I believe that even if my champion or momentum partner never mentions my name, when they nail their keynote, the organizer is going to remember who introduced them.

Starting to see the power of momentum partnerships?

GIVERS, TAKERS, AND BALANCE-SHEET MAKERS

As I began networking in earnest, I found that people could be categorized another way. I came to think of them as "givers," "takers," and "balance-sheet makers." While talking to my ghostwriter, Derek, who you might remember from chapter 10 of my previous book—where he came from behind the curtain and told his real story of rapid growth with sales—he snapped his fingers and said, "That sounds just like Adam Grant's model!" So of course I had to check it out. (Turns out he's also an introvert!)

In Adam Grant's book *Give and Take*, he similarly categorizes people as givers, takers, and matchers. Takers are exactly what they sound like: they take without ever giving much in return. Matchers, or what I call balance-sheet makers, basically keep a mental or physical ledger. They may do something for you, but they expect a favor of equal value to be returned to them at some point. The good news is, it works both ways: if you do a favor for them, they feel indebted to you until they can pay it back. The bad news is, like the people I met at that local speakers' group, they are often so worried about doing anything for you without getting something of equal benefit in return that they will likely not take the lead in any exchange of value.

You can't have lasting, long-term momentum partner or champion relationships with takers. You'll get sucked dry! While they'll accept value in any form, they're unlikely to ever reciprocate. You also can't really have good, healthy relationships with momentum partners or champions that are balance-sheet makers. They'll always be keeping score, eventually becoming either nervous because they owe you or angry because they feel you owe them. If you're like me, you'll find these types of relationships way too stressful to maintain.

The only momentum partner or champion relationships that last the test of time are with those who are givers. Givers are people who simply offer value without worrying about the ledger. For me and my prized relationships, like Judy Robinett (momentum partner) and Gerhard Gschwandtner (champion), we don't keep score. We don't keep a balance sheet. We simply try to help each other as much as we can—more often than not, without even being asked.

Take a second and ask yourself: Are you a giver? Are you a taker? Or are you a balance-sheet maker? For many, the first thing that comes to mind is, "I'd like to be a giver, but I have nothing to give." Of course, that's never really true. One thing I know for sure is that givers find a way.

Remember, with Judy, I didn't have the network that she did, but I hustled to support our newly established partnership. Luckily, she noticed.

But what about champions? What do we really have to offer these elite individuals?

What people at this level value most of all is authentic connection with no strings attached.

When you meet a potential champion, I'd recommend that you embrace my number one rule of networking—it's not about you! So many people get the opportunity to connect with champions but then destroy that opportunity by shooting off their resume or angling for a favor. When I meet a potential champion, I never push my own agenda. I focus on asking about them and what they're excited about. And, where I can, I go into value-delivery overdrive.

My good friend Jim Cathcart is a great example of this. He's become a long-term mentor to me, which of course I see as an honor. After all, he's basically speaking royalty. But Jim is a little old school when it comes to technology, so I volunteered some advice on how to automate and dominate on social media, hoping he'd find it valuable. I was happy to be helpful and give him as much time as he needed. To be honest, I would have been happy to pick up his dry cleaning, if he'd asked. That's how much I value my champion relationship with him.

When Jim learned I was launching my first book, he said, "Oh, that's exciting! Would it be helpful if I wrote a feature about it in *Top Sales World* magazine?" Would it!? As it turned out, he's known the publisher for decades. That write-up got me on their radar, and I was later named by them as one of the top fifty speakers in the world. In fact, I was on the cover of the magazine for their November 2019 edition. Wow! All of this came from a few conversations, offering advice where I could, sharing a few high-level media introductions, and having no agenda other than valuing his time. So much gained, including a friendship I'll value for life.

This was also true of Brian Smith, better known as the founder of the billion-dollar company UGG Boots. I mean, what could I possibly offer him?

As it turns out, Brian was an introvert looking to break into the speaking world himself. He'd hired many extroverted speaking coaches, all of whom left him feeling uncomfortable. I emboldened him to just be himself, tell more of his own personal stories, and be more authentic. I also made him the closing speaker at one of my events, and he absolutely nailed it! Brian has now gone on to become a sought-after speaker; as I write this, he just got a standing ovation as the keynote at the Inc. 5000 conference.

I've found that even the most highly successful people still welcome advice and assistance in areas outside of their expertise—as long as it doesn't come with a catch. Of course, Brian didn't really need my help to succeed in the speaking world. Just as Jim would have likely mastered social media on his own. They're both business titans who've built their careers on finding a way. Yet they still welcomed and appreciated my support.

Treasure your champion contacts. Be sure to always be giving and rarely, if ever, asking.

HOW I LEARNED TO NETWORK

I have a confession to make. I originally learned how to foster relationships with champion connections, not in the world of business, but by getting into bars and nightclubs when I was barely in my twenties.

At a friend's housewarming, I happened to make the acquaintance of Michele Phyman, the head promoter for one of the most exclusive clubs in Melbourne back then, called Boutique. When I say exclusive, I mean there were long lines out the door, the wait was well over an hour, they wouldn't let more than two guys in together, and they often declined you outright.

During the housewarming, I told Michele stories and offered to introduce her to some of my business contacts. At the end of the evening, she invited me to her club.

On an off night, I went with a friend and waited in line. When we got inside, I found her and said hello. She responded, "Why didn't you call? I would have come down to get you."

"I didn't want to impose," I explained.

As the evening progressed, I made sure to keep circling back with Michele, engaging in conversation but being careful not to take too much of her time. Before I left for the night, I went to say goodbye. She said to me, "In the future, make sure you call me whenever you're downstairs. I don't want you having to wait in line again!" Which, of course, I sincerely thanked her for.

The next time I went back, I had a drink with her. I asked her about her life; she talked about her son and the trouble he was getting into. I offered advice and ideas where welcomed. Michele asked about me—if I'd met a girl yet and how my business was doing. She seemed to love hearing my stories about a kid in his early twenties (who just two years ago was still in high school and working at McDonald's part-time) running a multimillion-dollar business and trying to figure it all out. Over time, we became great friends, and I would jokingly call her my club mum. We even went to dinner once a year and, always, I'd pay, just as a way to show gratitude and appreciation for her friendship.

I still remember the time I brought three of my mates to Boutique on a Saturday night. I grew up with some really rough friends. They had tattoos up and down their arms, one even had a tattoo on the side of his neck, and they all towered over me. (Not hard to do. For someone with my frame, you certainly feel safer going out with a couple of hulking bruisers around you.)

The security guys eyed my three friends as they said, "Four guys, no girls, and tattoos? No way, you'll need to go somewhere else."

We walked away and I texted Michele a low-key message about being outside, any chance she could help? And no problem if she was busy or the club was packed out. I got a text back within minutes that said, "Wait there." She came out, yelled at the bouncers for not letting me in, and told them she didn't care how many people I had with me, I should never be turned away. One of the bouncers mentioned that my friend's neck tattoo was against club policy. She quickly grabbed the scarf from around her own neck, put it around my friend's, and personally led us in.

From then on, security just let me do whatever I wanted. One time, after a good friend's birthday, I had twenty mates with me—twenty!—and they simply unhooked the rope and let us all file past the line, no girls with us, no questions asked.

If I'd had my three categories of people back then, Michele would definitely have fit in the champion category. I'm on a different mission now (and I've grown up—I can't remember the last time I went to a club). My focus has changed and, therefore, so have my champions and momentum partners.

But do you see how you treat champions differently than your prospects and momentum partners? They're not people to immediately profit from but relationships to continually invest in with advice, gratitude, and time.

DO YOUR RESEARCH BEFORE YOU GET IN THE ROOM

Before heading into an event, wouldn't it be nice to know who's going to be there? Wouldn't it be great to already have multiple conversations started so that, when you show up, you could just continue them? Wouldn't that take the pressure off?

In 2014, when I first came to Austin, I realized I needed to get serious about networking. I didn't want to just show up at events and hope for the best. I didn't want to walk out thinking, "Networking doesn't work," or "I just wasn't lucky today."

In this digitally connected world, there had to be a smarter way.

I decided to do a little online research to uncover what events my niche prospects, possible momentum partners, and possible champions might be frequenting. Within minutes I'd discovered a monthly social event for small-business owners and community supporters, put on by a local coworking space called Capital Factory.

From there, I discovered Capital Factory had a Facebook members group. After joining, I checked who'd gone last month. It was easy; several people had posted photos at the event, so all I had to do was look at the profiles of anyone tagged. I then searched those names and matched the faces on LinkedIn.

After checking out each profile and deciding whom I wanted to connect with, I sent them each a short message that said: "Great to virtually meet you! I'm new to Austin and heard that the Capital Factory mixer is a great place to connect with people supporting the small-business community, which I'm really passionate about supporting myself. I saw that you've attended that event in the past. Would you recommend it?"

One of the people I connected with was Thom Singer, the only Certified Professional Speaker in Austin (CSP is the highest designation awarded by the National Speakers Association, or NSA). He shot me back a message saying, "Absolutely! I can't accept your connection request though. I only accept those after, at least, a coffee?"

"Let's do it!" I immediately replied. When we met up, I reiterated that I'd just moved to Austin and told him that, as I was relaunching my speaking business in the US, I was looking to become part of a speaking community.

He said, "You know what? Come to our next NSA Austin mastermind event as my guest, and I'll introduce you to everyone."

True to his word, when I saw him at the event, he came over, shook my hand like we were old friends, and introduced me around the room. I now have many clients and some very supportive friends from the NSA. Sure, I may have eventually gotten them on my own, but being introduced by one of the most respected members of the group gave me automatic standing right out of the gate. (A few years later, Thom was actually one of the committee members who voted on me being a CSP myself, Austin's second. We're still friends to this day.)

From another tagged photo, I learned of a person who was an organizer for Austin's Google Startup Weekend. I messaged her on LinkedIn, talking about what I'd done in Australia and my love for giving back to new entrepreneurs. She never messaged back . . . but when I showed up at the next

Capital Factory event, she recognized me, and we started a great discussion. Then she walked me over to Sean Duffy, the host of the entire event. From there, Sean invited me to be a judge at Austin's Google Startup Weekend.

During my initial research, I also discovered one of the most frequented Meetup events in Austin, called TechMap. Meetup and other networking platforms often have people's social media profiles linked to the app. Following the links, I identified some potentially great contacts. There was one in particular I wanted to meet: Johan Borge, the person who founded the event. He accepted my connection request.

After hearing about my desire to give back, Johan asked me to speak at his event. This later turned into judging another business competition, a developer hackathon called Angel-Hack.

In less than twelve months, I was invited to events as one of the most connected people in the city. My network included the mayor, city officials, the governor's office, local officials from the Small Business Administration, executives at VC firms, the founders or managers of all the big coworking facilities, senior leaders of Austin-based corporations, nonprofit lenders, senior faculty of Austin universities, and most of the big names in the small-business space.

I share all of this with you not to brag but to show you how simple it was for me. I did just a little online sleuthing, identified high-potential individuals, reached out to them beforehand, and then picked up the conversation when we met in person. That, combined with the other tactics in this book, and I was ready to rock the networking room. Soon, you will be too!

That's strategic networking.

Today, with social media, networking websites, and apps, there is a wealth of personal information out there—our "cyber footprint," if you will. People post pictures of themselves at events, they like and comment, they promote things they're going to, their friends and colleagues tag them . . . and it's all just waiting for you to discover.

And from these social profiles, you can usually guess if the potential connection is more likely to be a prospect, momentum partner, or champion. Do they have a podcast? Are they a big deal at their company (or in general)? Have they written a book? Are they on any leadership committees? Do they run events of their own? Are they part of elite clubs? Do they volunteer anywhere?

Every time I consider skipping the sleuthing phase of my networking efforts, I'm reminded of what a friend of mine once told me. I happened to run into her at an event, just as it was getting started. One of the first things she said was, "I'm sorry to tell you this, but if you're here to sell something, you're wasting your time. There's no money in this room." She went on to explain that she'd been volunteering as the host of the event in the hopes of getting clients for the last six months and hadn't made a penny.

Well, after speaking to all the people I'd researched and connected with prior to the event, then running through my prepared statements (which you'll learn in the next chapter), I'd made several sales appointments, resulting in thousands of dollars from a room with "no money." I was also invited to speak at another event (by a newfound champion) and was offered a few introductions (from a newfound momentum partner). These Schrödinger-cat opportunities were in front of my acquaintance the whole time. But because she was an aimless, nonstrategic networker, she had convinced herself that everyone there was cheap. The money was there; she was just saying the wrong things or speaking to the wrong people!

So, the next time you plan to go to a networking event or conference, go online first. If you were selling to a board of directors or interviewing with a group of executives, would you research them first? Of course you would! Well, networking should be no different.

I remember after speaking at an Intel event, an attendee approached me to say hello. We talked about storytelling for a while, then he transitioned into him being an introvert and hating small talk. He said, "I usually can't just start talking to someone, but approaching you was easy. After seeing you speak today, I feel like I know you and can talk to you about your subject matter. But I just can't network with other people here, as I don't know them well enough and have nothing of substance to talk about with them."

His comment perplexed me. At this particular event, eighty-five of Intel's most senior sales and marketing leaders were in attendance. Many of these people had been with the company for decades, not to mention they had been flying across the world to attend it for years.

I asked him, "Did you have an idea who was coming? Could you have gotten a list of attendees in advance?"

He thought for a second. "Sure, yeah."

"Could you have checked out those people online and connected with them via LinkedIn or some other networking platform before coming? Perhaps checked out what they were posting about?"

Again, yes.

"Then there's really nothing stopping you from networking with people inside your own company. Next time, go pick the titles or divisions of people that you'd like to meet. Look at what they're posting on their social profiles. Where did they go to school? Are they sharing any articles of interest? Then, check to see if they have a personal profile with public posts."

I continued, "For example, I know a senior VP at Dell Technologies. Every day, he posts something about his new obsession, Peloton biking. Imagine if I were a Peloton biker, too, and dropped that into the conversation when we met. *Your* potential contacts are doing the same thing, posting articles about projects they're working on, a charity they care about, a book they enjoyed. All you need to say is, 'Looking forward to meeting you,' and then ensuring that topic comes up."

To underscore the point, and to show him how fruitful this strategy can be, I shared a personal example. When I spoke at the American Association of Inside Sales Professionals (AA-ISP), my team and I connected with every single VP in attendance. For every one of them within driving distance of the Raleigh-Durham Triangle, where I now live, we arranged coffees locally before the event. For everyone else, we set up meetings at the event. I barely had a moment to myself because of all the people we'd scheduled me to catch up with! (We might have overdone it a little. I'm trying to learn to slow down.)

Within weeks of the event, I'd closed tens of thousands of dollars of business with a large medical supply company and a big telecom, received an introduction to one of the world's largest speaking bureaus that soon booked me for a five-figure keynote, and walked out with multiple new champions who have already led to customers, speaking events, and public endorsements of my work.

All because I networked *before* going into the room.

Don't be afraid to connect with ten or twenty people leading up to your event. Focus on champions first, momentum partners second, and prospects or employers third. Remember, one champion or momentum partner can get you in front of dozens, hundreds, or even thousands of prospects or employers. They're the key to changing your life.

Okay, now it's time to discover exactly what to say when you get there.

7

what to do in the room

We are what we repeatedly do.
Excellence, then, is not an act,
but a habit.

—WILL DURANT, *The Story of Philosophy*

Have you ever seen the movie *Groundhog Day*?

If so, you'll remember that Phil Connors (played by Bill Murray, who, surprisingly, is also an introvert) was forced to relive the same day over and over again and that he decided to use his repetitive existence to woo his coworker Rita Hanson (played by Andie MacDowell). He spent weeks trying to have the perfect date, attempting to say and do all the right things. He went through trial and error, suggesting different activities, using different lines, and finding out her favorite things to do. He even learned new skills, like ice sculpting and playing the piano. He kept what worked and tried something different when things went wrong. (Of course, you might also recall, none of this worked for Phil until he became a better human being—something I'm sure is unnecessary for you!)

Groundhog Day serves as a great analogy for one of the key ideas of my networking approach: focus on the system, not the conversation. Phil kept repeating the same dialogue and the same activities with Rita, changing one small thing each time, determining whether that change got him closer to or further from his goal. That's the same mind-set I want you to have when you walk into a networking room. You shouldn't worry about hitting a home run in your first or even tenth conversation. If that happens, which it just may, that's a bonus. For now, I just want you to focus on having a more structured conversation. Hone that conversation each day, just as if you were in *Groundhog Day*.

That's the real magic of my system. It's the key not only to wooing your prospects, momentum partners, and champions but leaving them in awe.

PREPARE FOR NETWORKING SUCCESS

Growing up, everyone told me I had dyslexia. Luckily, thanks to the unrelenting efforts of my mother, I was diagnosed with a visual processing disorder called Irlen Syndrome. The good news was, by just wearing a pair of colored lenses, I could finally start the process of learning to read. The bad news was, it also led to everyone in class incessantly teasing the boy with funny glasses. Add to that, I had awful acne. I still remember the day I was playing basketball and the ball hit me in the head, popping one of my pimples. The ridicule of my classmates hurt more than the hit.

To say that these years eroded my self-confidence would be an understatement. It was hard enough for me to speak even to my few friends, much less a stranger.

But today, I see those adversities as the seeds of my success. My lack of confidence, combined with my determination to excel in spite of it, led me to handle social encounters very differently—in a way that felt right for me.

When I found something that worked—a way to greet people, a rapport builder people always seemed to like—I clung to it for dear life and used it every time. And a funny thing happened along the way. The more I used what worked, the more comfortable I became in its delivery. The more confident I grew, the easier, smoother, and more polished my delivery became. It wasn't long before I began connecting with people more easily and more quickly.

I had discovered something extraordinary: that I could have the same conversation over and over, while for the person I spoke to, it felt like the first time.

Imagine having the same conversation a hundred times. Don't you think you'd be even better at it the hundred and first? Of course you would. Even if only 80 percent went according to plan, don't you think you'd feel more relaxed and able to guide the other 20 percent more effectively?

Think about it: When do you usually mess up? When you're the most nervous, right? We introverts tend to overthink things. I know I sure do! We get stuck in our own heads trying to work out what to say. By the time we do, the moment has passed. When you're asked a question you weren't expecting, when someone says a joke you weren't ready for, when you force yourself to strike up a conversation, when someone reacts poorly to what you do for a living (like my neighbor the gym owner)—your lizard brain goes into fight-or-flight mode. You're not thinking straight because a big portion of your brain's focus is readying your body to fight or flee.

When I'm out socializing with family or friends, even today, I sometimes jumble my words or get stuck in my head—and that's okay. In fact, when it's just my wife and me at home, it happens all the time. Brittany and I even have a running joke about it. When I notice, or she points it out, I just laugh and say, "I'm a professional speaker!"

But the funny thing is, this very rarely happens in the networking room.

Once you've got your system down, you'll never really need to change it again. If you're always in the same rooms with the same types of people (your niche), and have already chosen the people to speak to (by doing your research), then the questions they ask, statements they make, and even jokes they tell will be mostly the same. This means that you'll always know exactly what you're going to say—though to your listener, it feels like a natural, organic conversation.

To get to this level of success, you need to perfect what I call your "Networking Playbook"—that is, scripting out what you actually plan to say.

If you've read my first book, then you will have already embraced the power of scripting. For those new to my work, you're likely thinking what a lot of my clients and students say out loud when I bring up the idea: "Matthew, I want to be authentic with people. The last thing I want is to come off sounding scripted."

If this is you, I totally understand where you're coming from. The last thing I'd ever want is for someone to feel I wasn't being real with them. My whole brand is built on authenticity—and, likely, so is yours.

But let me ask you a question, the same one I always ask when someone expresses a concern with scripting: "What's your favorite movie?"

One of my clients once responded with *Gangs of New York.*

I said, "Wow, I love that movie! Isn't Leonardo DiCaprio fantastic?" (Leo's another introvert, by the way.) "He's just so natural, isn't he?"

"Yes! He just embodies his part!"

"You know he's using a script, right?"

I received a puzzled look.

I went on, "DiCaprio didn't approach it like a telemarketer would and just read directly from a script. He memorized his lines and practiced until his delivery was so smooth that it looks like he's speaking naturally. You can achieve the exact same success with scripting a real conversation."

Then I shared my other big scripting discovery: knowing what you're going to say before heading into the networking room actually lets you be *more* authentic and natural, not less. It allows you to calm down and be totally present in the discussion.

After all, when you're meeting with a complete stranger for the first time, don't you always worry about whether you're saying the right thing? Aren't you often so focused on getting your own words right that you sometimes miss what the other person says? Don't you think it would remove a lot of that stress and worry if you already knew what you intended to say?

Whenever I share this, I'm always reminded of another movie, *Hitch*, in which Will Smith is a love doctor who coaches guys on how to woo the woman of their dreams. In one scene, Hitch says, "Does it ever occur to women that maybe a guy might like to have a plan, you know, because he's nervous? He's not sure that he could just walk up to you and you'd respond if he said, 'I like you, I like you, I like you!'"

Of course, I'm not suggesting that you script your next date—though I've personally found that a little planning really helps there too. I'm telling you that the more prepared you are, the better you'll feel going into a networking discussion, knowing your lines and playing your part. Be real, but be prepared.

HOW TO INVITE CONVERSATIONS

Through the previous chapters, you've already uncovered all the necessary ingredients for your Networking Playbook. All you need is the recipe for how they all go together, in a way that feels congruent and authentic to you.

As you'll remember from chapter 5, I always try to be the first to ask, "So, what is it you do?" I listen intently, empathize, and ask genuine questions. With all my focus on them, at some point, they'll want to reciprocate and ask what I do. All I do is wait for their invitation, and then *bang*!—I press "play" on my internal tape player.

Here's the basic script I provide my clients:

"I'm the [insert UM]."
They ask: "The [UM]? What exactly is that?"
"Thanks for asking!"
[Share concise statement, drawing from your passion, your new understanding of your niche, and the three main problems you solve or outcomes you provide for them.]
Option 1: "Well, I hate seeing [niche] [define problems].
Option 2: "I love seeing [niche] [define success]; however, I find that [define problems].

"Do you know anyone like that?"

[Wait for response, which is almost always yes—especially if you've done all the right research beforehand.]

"Well, I'm on a mission to help [niche] realize/achieve/overcome/avoid [pleasure of attaining it or pain of not attaining it]. Not by [what most people are doing] but instead focusing on three often neglected/forgotten/ridiculously simple steps."

[Act like you're going to explain, then interrupt yourself.]

"Actually, you know what? Let me give you an example. See, when I first met [tell story]."

Finish with moral, then: "Does that make sense?"

[Wait for response.]

To bring it all together for you, here's what I say when people invite me to explain what I do as the Rapid Growth Guy:

Option 1: "Well, I hate seeing introverted small-business owners, with strong functional skills, constantly stuck in a hamster wheel of struggling to find interested prospects, set themselves apart, and make the sale, all while feeling like they're selling to prospects who only seem to care about one thing—price. Do you know anyone like that?"

Option 2: "Well, I love seeing introverted individuals with enough skill, passion, talent, and belief in themselves to launch their own business. However, I find that many of them end up stuck in an endless hamster wheel of struggling to find interested prospects, set themselves apart, and make the sale. Do you know anyone like that?"

Of course they do. That describes virtually everyone in or associated with my niche.

I then say, "I'm on a mission to help these business owners realize they don't need to give up on their dream business—that there is a way they can earn a phenomenal income doing what they love. Not by getting better at their functional skill, as they're usually already great at that, but instead by focusing on three often neglected steps. Actually, you know what, let me give you an example. See, when Wendy"—or Whitney or Derek—"first came to me . . ."

At the end, after sharing my moral, when I say, "Does that make sense?" most people say, "Yes, that's me! I need what Wendy has!" or "I have the exact same problems that Wendy did!" or "Wow, you really know your stuff. I'm not a small-business owner myself, but I want to introduce you to—"

See, they've just experienced a powerful cocktail of passion, mission, and story. They've heard the enthusiasm in my voice and felt my excitement. How could they not be affected by it? If they were one of my potential niche prospects, momentum partners, or champions, how could they not be compelled to further the relationship?

Here's the truth: as I touched on in the preceding chapters, most people go days, weeks, months, or even years without being around someone who just lights them up. If you can do that for them, even for a second, wow!—they'll want to stay connected to that energy.

Now, if you're like many people, you might be wondering, "Will people really listen for that long?" My experience over thousands of conversations of my own and the collective conversations of my clients and students is, unequivocally, yes!

It works for several reasons. First, it's not as though you're just talking at them; the script is designed to be a two-way dialogue. Second, thanks to the power of your Unified Message, they asked you for more information. You're not shoving something down their throat, you're simply explaining because they asked. Third, because of the genuine interest you showed in them, they want to show you a similar courtesy. Fourth, if you've done your research correctly, you are speaking to those in or associated with your niche, which means that what you're saying directly applies to them or people they know well. Fifth, as soon as you begin telling a story, their mirror neurons begin firing as their brains go, "Story time!"

Remember: most people are not very good at networking. So even if you do this in a way that is less than perfect, it will still be a whole lot better than the transactional pitchers out there or the unplanned, aimless time wasters.

You might even find that people want to hire you right there on the spot—which sounds ideal, right? But let's see why that can actually present a problem, and what to do when it happens.

DON'T TRY TO LAND THE DEAL

Several years ago, while volunteering at a business support event in Austin, I met Gavin and Ray, who had just purchased a sales-training franchise.

At the event, the owners of each small business received fifteen minutes of advice from each mentor. Before I was even halfway through my fifteen-minute allotment with Gavin and Ray, they asked if I'd consider working with them—immediately inquiring about price.

Of course, I would have loved to jump on the opportunity, especially as this was back when I was still new to the US and trying to get my brand off the ground. But instead, I said, "I'm honored that you're open to the possibility of working with me further. I have no doubt I could help; however, today I'm here with a 'give back' focus. Having a sales conversation with you now, in this safe environment, would feel like an abuse of trust. I'd love to discuss the possibility at another time, if you're open to it?"

Of course, they agreed.

We booked a meeting time for the following day and, by the end of that meeting, we agreed to work together. But here's the cool thing: they had spoken on the way home and decided to work with me as long as the engagement was around $10,000. They also commented on how much trust and respect I had fostered by not immediately pouncing on the chance to work together, which solidified my value in their minds. In short: my willingness to say "not now," in a way that made it all about them, led to the sale.

No matter how tempting it is, if someone says they want to work with you, don't try to land the deal in the room. A networking event is not the place to start talking particulars. You're going to be rushed, you're going to get interrupted, and it can get just plain uncomfortable. Instead, respond with something like, "I'm honored that you're open to the possibility of working with me. However, this is not really the best forum for me to fully understand your needs. If you're open to it, I'd love to set up a quick call/Zoom meeting/coffee/lunch next week/month to discuss the possibility further. Would that work for you?"

Remember, the goal is to get the deal. And the best chance of that is with a scheduled meeting outside the networking room.

END WITH A PLAN

So what happens when someone *doesn't* immediately ask about hiring or buying from you? How do you bring a great conversation to a successful conclusion?

You've gone through your entire script and story, ending with, "Does that make sense?" Now what?

After a little back-and-forth (which will also follow a predictable pattern the more you do it), you'll want to use what marketers define as a "call to action" (CTA). It's a series of phrases designed to elicit a desirable response. Having prepared and practiced CTAs will drastically improve your ability to turn a good discussion into a great outcome.

You need a separate CTA for potential prospects, momentum partners, and champions. Here is what I suggest for each group:

For potential champions, you can say, "[Name], I'm really enjoying this conversation; however, I don't want to monopolize your time if you have other people you need to chat with. How about I reach out via email to schedule a lunch or a coffee? Would that be something you'd be open to?" You might also offer to make an introduction or two, if it makes sense to do so.

If you've identified the person as a potential momentum partner, you can conclude by saying, "[Name], I'm really enjoying this conversation; however, I don't want to monopolize your time. Also, there are a few other people I promised I would say hello to while I was here. When I get back to the office, [I'll be sure to shoot you through those introductions I promised you, or I'm going to shoot through a few introductions I think might be helpful to you]—is that okay?"

Finally, if they are a potential prospect, and especially if they've shared similar problems to the ones you described in your story, you can offer a follow-up conversation. "If you're open to it, we can schedule a quick call/Zoom meeting/coffee/ lunch and I can talk you through the process I used to help Wendy. Would that be helpful?" (The key is to deliver this line like you're indifferent to the outcome. After all, you're just trying to be helpful.) By leading with an offer of free, targeted advice, you've fostered a great deal of trust, enough that many people will welcome your nonsalesy offer to help.

On accepting your offer for a follow-up conversation, you can respond with, "Terrific! Now, I know I'm booked solid for the next few days." Then, pull out your phone and say, "But, looking at my schedule, I could make next [day] morning at [time] or [day] afternoon at [time] work. Would either of those options work for you?" I always like to offer two different days of the week at two different times, one in the morning and the other in the afternoon. This changes their focus from thinking, "Do I really want to schedule right now?" to considering the best day and time instead.

(Now, I have one more trick that I use in every networking room, and it gives me excellent results with prospects: an offer to email free, valuable content to those not yet ready to commit to a further meeting. I simply offer it as an attempt to help them obtain the outcome themselves, but it also automates the whole follow-up hustle. If you already have free content, or are willing to create some, check the bonus section for further information.)

That's it. Those simple CTAs, along with your full script and stories, will grow your network quickly, reliably, and profitably.

Of course, regardless of who you're speaking with, not everything will go exactly as planned. But even if only 80 percent does, think of what that could do to your networking success.

Actually, let me give you an example to illustrate the difference.

A TALE OF TWO NETWORKERS

In doing my research before attending a conference, I opened up the events app provided by the organizers. It allowed me to see all the people who were attending or presenting at the event, along with their positions and one-click access to their LinkedIn profiles. As I've suggested you should do, I started connecting with anyone I saw as a potential champion or momentum partner. One of the people I reached out to was Tom Dekle, a senior IBM executive who I noticed lived in the same city as I did—Chapel Hill, North Carolina. From his LinkedIn profile, I also noticed that he was the recipient of a lifetime achievement award in sales.

He never responded.

At the event, though, when I walked past him, it was clear he recognized me. While this might seem like a chance encounter, even a very lucky one, remember Louis Pasteur's thoughts on chance: it favors the prepared mind.

While most people go to an event and find a place to sit, stand, or even hide, I walk through the room, looking for faces I recognize or smiles and eye contact from people who recognize me. Often within minutes, this leads to a "chance" encounter. The key to doing this well is casually walking from place to place, always looking like you're heading somewhere but are in no rush to get there. I often walk from the bar to the bathroom, then to the catering station, and then, if needed, even outside, like I'm planning to make a phone call, until that chance encounter happens. Needless to say, in a small room, you can only do this once or twice before it looks strange. But if you've connected with people beforehand, I've found it never takes that long. Worst case, after going outside, time your entrance back into the room with someone else. Open the door for them and say something like, "So you made it just in time, too, huh?" That should be all you need to get a conversation started.

Initially, I was able to identify Tom only as a familiar face. After all, I'd connected with many people before the event, and he never responded. But after he introduced himself, I realized who I was speaking with and remembered that we both lived in Chapel Hill.

We began chatting about the city and discovered our wives liked the same bookstores, that we all liked some of the same foodie-type restaurants, and that we loved Fearrington Village. We then began talking business, which of course led to me showing interest in him and all the things he was doing. It wasn't long before I got to share my UM, passion, and mission.

Finally I said, "Tom, I'm really enjoying this conversation; however, I don't want to monopolize your time if you have other people you need"—key word, *need*—"to chat with. I can have my assistant reach out, and maybe I can take you to lunch when we're back in Chapel Hill?" (You'll recognize this line as my CTA for potential champions.)

By being prepared to disengage, I signaled that I was being respectful of his time, not a potential clinger. It said, "We're equals. We're peers. I'd like to establish a real and authentic relationship. I'm not looking for anything for myself. There's no sales pitch here." It also ensured I didn't overstay my welcome. I gave him an easy way out, to say, "Thank you, Matthew, I really appreciate that. Enjoy the rest of the conference."

Instead, he said, "No, no, Matthew—I'm really enjoying our conversation. Unless you have somewhere else to be, I'd love to continue it."

Great! Now, I had his permission to continue.

Fast-forward ten minutes. As we were speaking, I watched a guy quickly walk in the ballroom, look around, spot us, and make a beeline for us. "Hey, guys, I don't really know anyone here," he said. "Mind if I join you for a while?"

Unfortunately, unbeknownst to him, he'd already started things off on the wrong foot. When two people are clearly engaged in a closed conversation, that is, standing directly face-to-face as Tom and I were, that's a signal that they don't want to be interrupted. This is what my good friend and champion Ivan Misner would call a closed group. (Google Ivan's name and "Open vs. Closed Networking" to see some great diagrams.)

He then asked, "What do you two do?" After we briefly replied, he followed up with, "Great! I sure could use your advice. Can I ask you some questions?" He then launched into a fifteen-minute Q&A. Tom and I both answered his questions and gave freely. But it was a little awkward, as I think we both felt interrupted from the great conversation we were already having. Eventually, there was an awkward pause and the interloper saw it as his signal to leave.

(I have to admit, I've made these mistakes myself more than once, so my heart did go out to the guy.)

Once he'd left, Tom and I went back to enjoying our discussion. We chatted for about fifteen more minutes before I moved into another prepared statement: "Tom, I am loving this discussion; however, it looks like catering is coming to an end, and you'll never forgive me if you go hungry tonight. I must admit, I'm starving too. How about I buy you a coffee in a few weeks and we can chat further?"

Why did I say this, when things were going so well?

Remember: I like to leave discussions on a high note. After all, that's the best chance you'll get of a follow-up meeting, right?

Tom responded, "Yes, that would be great! Let's do it!"

Later that night, I did what I call my "last lap." At a formal networking event, when I feel things are coming to an end, I make it a point to walk around the event space one last time. Just like when I arrive, I walk casually around the room, but this time I'm only looking for people making direct eye contact. Often, they're someone that I chatted with earlier, someone I'd connected with before the event but not yet spoken to, or someone who'd overheard me talking with someone else. Usually, they say something like, "I was hoping I'd run into you before you left." Then they either ask a follow-up question or ask if we can schedule a call to chat further. I'm often surprised at how many deals result from my last lap before heading home to collapse.

As "luck" would have it, I walked past Tom and two other IBM executives heading toward the door.

"Matthew!" he said. "We were just leaving. Why don't you come join us for a drink?"

Wow, what a great opportunity! Being invited out for drinks by one of IBM's senior VPs and a lifetime sales achievement recipient! With two other high-level execs to boot!

I politely turned him down.

"Thank you so much for such a kind offer. I'd love to; however, I have another massive day tomorrow, and I won't be my best if I don't get some downtime. Can I take a rain check?"

"Of course," Tom replied. "I look forward to catching up with you in Chapel Hill soon."

When I got back to my hotel room, I connected with the other two IBM execs on LinkedIn, thanking them for the invitation. Then, I sent a message to Tom apologizing for not being able to join them but that my assistant would reach out ASAP to help us get a coffee scheduled.

Ever since, Tom has been an incredible friend and supportive champion of my work (he was even kind enough to provide an endorsement for this book). In another event we both attended, a much smaller and local venue this time, Tom gave me a glowing endorsement, and I picked up a medical supply company as a client that I likely wouldn't have otherwise, worth more than $20,000 for just the first engagement.

Now, contrast my approach with the guy who did zero research, had no idea who either I or Tom was, walked up to a closed conversation, and turned the discussion to himself for fifteen minutes.

Regardless of intent, he signaled to us that he was out for himself, a transactional taker. Sadly, without understanding why, he likely walked out thinking, "Networking doesn't work," or "I just wasn't lucky today."

On the other hand, I approached the event as a strategic giver and left with multiple highly placed executive contacts and several prospects.

This is why I say that 90 percent of networking success happens outside the room. If you focus on the system, not the individual conversation, and you do your homework before showing up, then being in the room itself is easy. Suddenly you'll be a lot, lot "luckier."

PRACTICE, PRACTICE, PRACTICE

How can you get your anxiety down and your confidence up when networking? How do you deliver a networking script without sounding or feeling inauthentic?

You need to practice.

The good news is, learning your script and delivering it in a natural way won't take anywhere near as long as you'd expect.

Let me break it down into three steps:

1. Narrative Chaining: The process of memorizing your script and stories.
2. Imagination: Visualizing yourself delivering your networking script.
3. Buddying Up: Role-playing with someone you trust, to ensure your delivery is clear and to uncover anything you may have missed.

Let's look at each of these steps in more detail.

Narrative Chaining

Have you ever seen a stage actor deliver an engaging monologue? When done well, you can't help being amazed at the actor's ability to deliver lines and lines of text while acting out a scene.

Fortunately, remembering your networking script is going to be much easier than that. You don't need to be an actor. You just need to practice how to talk about yourself, your passion, your mission, and a story of someone you really helped.

While most people have no problem memorizing the initial portion of their networking script, memorizing their three stories can feel a bit daunting. After all, they're usually several pages long and full of emotional content they want to get right.

But I promise you, it really is simple.

Here's how I memorized my first story:

First, I printed it out in size 18 font, which took almost four full pages, and summarized each paragraph into one, two, or three one-to-four-word bullet points—just enough to jog my memory. I read the first paragraph a few times and then tried to say it out loud using just the bullet points I'd created as a guide. If I got stuck and the bullet points didn't help me, I revised and perfected them.

Once I could recite the first paragraph without the aid of the bullet points, I moved to the next and did the same thing. When I could recite the second paragraph without looking at my notes, I tried to say the two paragraphs together. I'd usually need a bullet point prompt once or twice, but I was soon able to recite the two paragraphs together from memory. Then I moved to the third paragraph, fourth paragraph, and so on. It only took about two hours until I could recite the entire story completely from memory.

That's it. You just need this simple process, a few hours, and a willingness to practice.

Important note: As you're learning your script, you'll get stuck from time to time, and that's okay. When this happens, though, don't ad-lib to fill in the gaps. Doing this makes it nearly impossible to remember your networking script the way you originally wrote it—which is the most concise and best possible way.

So if you get stuck or find yourself inventing details, you must stop and get back on track. Take a breath and see if the correct words come to you. If not, check the part you missed, practice that part again, and then recite everything from the top. It can get a little tedious sometimes, especially if you make a mistake in one of the later paragraphs. But it's only a matter of time till everything rolls off your tongue. So stick with it!

Your Imagination Is Your Friend

In my late twenties, in an attempt to better understand language and thought as well as its effect on emotions and behaviors, I signed up for a neuro-linguistic programming (NLP) training course.

During the training, Brad Greentree, one of our instructors, told us a story about his old scuba diving training business and how it was saved through the power of imagination.

He shared that, before his surprise discovery, he would sign up a whole group of new trainees, get them to put their gear on, take them out on his boat, and then ask them, one at a time, to dive into the water. Now, if you've ever gone scuba diving, then you know how unnatural it feels to stick your head underwater and continue breathing. As someone with a diver's license myself, I can attest to how disconcerting it can feel—especially when diving off a boat for the first time. You worry about hitting your head, you have your *Oh, crap!* moment when you hit the water, and you're disoriented, all the while having to remind yourself that it's okay to breathe.

Frequently, he'd have someone panic after hitting the water, and to calm the person down, he'd have to take them back to shore. Since he was a solo act, this meant that everybody had to get back in the boat and head back too. What made matters worse was, the chances of someone else freaking out almost doubled when the group finally arrived back for a second attempt. They'd all seen the other person panic, then had to sit there for the half-hour trip—imagination running wild—thinking of what it would be like when it was their turn. (Your imagination can work for you or against you.)

His first solution was to hire someone else to come with them, so that he could continue scuba diving with the group while his employee took the panicked person back to shore. But then he was barely making any money.

It was around that time that he crossed paths with an NLP coach, who suggested an unlikely solution.

He said, "On the way out to the dive location, have the group close their eyes and imagine diving off the side of the boat. Then have them think about swimming with the fish, touching the sandy bottom, and gazing at the coral before finally getting back on the boat to high-five one another and celebrate an awesome experience." Finally, he suggested getting them to imagine the whole scenario at least one more time before dropping anchor to dive.

Brad told us, "It worked!" He rarely had someone freak out again.

Why did this work? Because our minds can't tell the difference between a real and an imagined scenario. As far as the divers' lizard brains and limbic systems were concerned, they'd already successfully flipped off the boat at least twice before.

I use this same type of visualization trick when I speak at events. When I notice my nerves acting up, I imagine myself walking onstage, having everyone hanging on my every word, and as I say my last sentence, everyone rising up to give me a cheering standing ovation. Then I imagine myself walking off with a smile, going back to my hotel room, and jumping up and down to celebrate, like a kid whose parents just told them they're going to Disney World.

I do the same for networking. Before I get out of my car, I close my eyes and imagine walking into the networking room. I visualize entering the doors and, within minutes, running into a potential champion I'd been hoping to see. Then a possible momentum partner. Then a possible prospect. Just before leaving, when doing my last lap, I imagine seeing someone signaling for me to come over. When I walk over to them, they tell me they'd overheard my discussion with someone else and ask if I'm open to booking a call to talk further. Finally, I imagine leaving the event to get back into my car, look down at all the cards I've received and review all the meetings I've booked. Before opening my eyes, I take the time to embrace what I'm feeling—which is usually pumped and excited!

Whenever I do this, I feel the anxiety, stress, and worry just melt away.

But the usefulness of the imaginative process extends far beyond simply keeping your emotions at bay. It can be an incredibly effective tool when practicing your networking script. Once you know your script well, close your eyes and imagine walking into the room, having conversations with possible prospects, momentum partners, and champions. Imagine all the dialogue, especially the dialogue before and after your scripted remarks. Anything that you imagine that comes up, that you don't have prepared remarks for—which will likely be a lot at first—take the time to open your eyes and script out and memorize a great response. Then close your eyes and start again.

Soon you'll have an answer for everything. You'll not only feel more confident in your ability to network, as your brain will have experienced success many times over, but you'll actually be more equipped to handle anything that comes at you.

However, before you run into the room, there's one more thing I'd like you to do.

Buddying Up

Once I feel I'm totally ready, I'll ask my wife, a colleague, one of my staff, one of my parents, or a friend to role-play with me, going easy on me at first, then later trying to catch me off guard. This helps me practice my flow and pacing. It also helps me uncover any further scenarios that I don't currently have a planned response for.

When you do this, remember to take the time to explain your niche, in detail, to whomever is assisting you. I go so far as to give them a real character to act out. That way, the questions they'll ask will be as close to the real thing as possible.

If you follow this advice, with just a few hours of preparation, you'll accomplish more in your next networking event than you accomplished in the last twenty!

Yes, it will take work. Yes, it will push you out of your comfort zone.

But it's your ticket to getting paid what you're worth and to attaining the respect that you deserve.

Take the time and get it right.

8

the step everyone forgets

Long-term consistency trumps
short-term intensity.
—attributed to BRUCE LEE

Have you ever been to a farmers' market?

You can't help thinking of the months and months of work that went into all that beautiful, fresh produce.

Can you imagine having to plow all those fields, till all that soil, and then during spring planting season, get all those seeds in the ground? But the work doesn't stop there. For the entire growing season, you then have to ensure all the crops get the water and nutrients they need to thrive. Finally comes harvest, and you have to head out again to gather your crops. Then and only then, you get to take them to market and *finally* cash in on all that hard work.

What do you think would happen if farmers didn't tend to their crops between planting season and harvest time? What if, during the entire growing season, they just left those seeds to grow on their own? No watering, no fertilizing, no nutrients—nothing. Do you think they'd have many crops come harvest? Maybe some, but nothing compared to the bounty that's possible with a little nurturing.

Networking without follow-up is like farmers neglecting to tend to their crops.

Sure, you'll get a few results, but without follow-up, you'll miss out on your biggest-yielding prospects, momentum partners, and champions—the relationships that require more time to grow.

Ask yourself: How many times have you sown seeds in the networking room, generated interest, then forgotten, ignored, or even avoided taking the time to water the crop? How many times have you arrived home with a stack of business cards, looked at each one, and thought:

"I had an awkward conversation with that person—we barely had enough to talk about. The last thing I want is a repeat of that. Sure, something might come of it, but I would be lucky if it did. So let's wait and see if they reach out to me." (They usually never do.)

"I think I convinced that person that what I do is interesting. Maybe I should contact them? But I don't want to impose . . . I'll just wait and let them make the next move." (They often don't.)

"I gave that person a ton of value, but they seemed to just expect me to help for free. Why doesn't anyone ever have the money to pay me?" (They probably did.)

"I got along with that person great. But I don't see anything of value there, other than cultivating a friendship. I'll just leave this one for now." (This may have been a great momentum partner.)

I get it. Until I learned to network the right way, I used to do and think the same things, and so did a lot of my clients.

Do you remember Jim Comer from chapter 2? How, after making the tough decision to focus solely on his speech writing and coaching business, he made $20,000 from a little focused effort?

Well, this success didn't come from cold-calling or networking for new prospects. It all came from just a little follow-up. See, in the weeks leading up to Christmas, Jim looked at his calendar and realized that bookings for the new year were looking dire. In fact, there wasn't a booking in sight.

Of course, this wasn't because he didn't deliver great outcomes. Jim is fantastic at what he does. Neither was it because he didn't go out networking, planting seeds any chance he'd get. It was because Jim was the world's worst at following up. He hates feeling as though he's imposing or being pushy. As such, he would almost always just wait and hope that people he'd connected with would follow up with him.

When they didn't, he'd tell himself all kinds of self-critical things like, "They probably went with somebody younger," or "I bet they thought I was too expensive."

But how could Jim possibly know if he didn't follow up? Maybe there was a family emergency. Maybe they threw their pants in the washer and forgot that his business card was in the pocket—I know I've done that more than once. Maybe somebody hacked their computer and they lost his email address. Or maybe they just got busy and put off the decision.

I said to Jim, "That's why it's so important that you follow up. Worrying all the time about imposing or being pushy is focusing your attention in the wrong direction. Sometimes a call, email, or social message is all they need to take positive action. Without your follow-up, they could stay stuck in an unhappy life or never get to achieve the results they know they deserve. You owe it to them—and to yourself—to do it."

Emboldened by my words, Jim finally said, "Okay, I'll do it. I'll reach out with an email or phone call to all the potential prospects I've spoken to recently and see what happens."

Within just a few hours, Jim's calendar looked totally different. Not only had he received confirmation from multiple groups that they'd like to book him for the new year, he was blown away by the responses. One replied almost instantly, saying, "Oh my gosh, I'm so glad you reached out! Our board decided unanimously that you'd be perfect for our event! Unfortunately, we had something crazy come up here and then none of us could find your details. We were about to have to start our search all over again! Yes, we would love to book you—are you still available?"

It's amazing what a little bit of follow-up can do!

Now, let's talk about what it looks like for champions, momentum partners, and prospects.

FOLLOW-UP FOR CHAMPIONS

For potential champions, I suggest you send them a simple email similar to the below:

[Name], it was a real honor speaking with you today and getting to hear about all the exciting things that you're working on. I was particularly inspired to hear [custom note about one specific thing that connects with your passion and mission or, as a last resort, something they were really excited about].

I was also happy to hear that you're open to continuing our discussion. Would any of the below times work for you? [Offer four time slots, two sooner and two later, and each set at a different time of day—morning or afternoon.]

Of course, it would be great to meet with you again in person, perhaps over coffee. However, if you're short on time, of course I'd settle for a voice or video call.

I look forward to hearing from you soon.

P.S. [If applicable] I've attached the [journal article, news report, statistic, book, or something that gives them value] that I told you about. I hope you find it as helpful/useful/inspiring as I did.

With everyone I meet (not just champions), if I haven't already, I connect with them via LinkedIn—today's professional platform of choice. I also follow them on any other social profiles I can find them on, hoping they'll follow back. For all my champions and momentum partners, I even send them a Facebook friend request. I do this with prospects, too, if I see they use it for business or feel they'd welcome the invitation.

On LinkedIn, I like to send the below personalized connection request, if we're not already connected. If we are, then I just send it as a personal message.

[Name], it was a real honor to meet you today, and I was excited to hear [similar custom note from email]. I just sent you an email with some time options to continue our discussion, did you get it okay? You never know with spam filters these days!

With champions, because they're so busy and in demand, I generally give them two to four weeks to respond. Then I follow up.

If, after a message or three, you don't get a response, don't get discouraged. You've likely done nothing wrong. You definitely shouldn't take it as a rejection. Many of these champions receive hundreds of emails and social messages a day, and many of the biggest influencers even purposely ignore messages, just to test you.

Jeffrey Gitomer is a great example of this.

Back in 2017, I'd just finished my first book and was on the hunt for high-level endorsements. Tim Burgard, my editor, suggested one person in particular. "I know he's not an introvert," Tim said, "but if you could get Jeffrey Gitomer—who wrote *The Little Red Book of Selling*—to endorse you, that would provide a huge amount of credibility."

"I don't know Jeffrey personally, but I'll find a way to make it happen," I replied.

I searched his name on LinkedIn and saw that we had a few connections in common. As a general rule, I find that if I can get three people to provide me with an introduction, I can almost always make the connection happen.

Unfortunately, after receiving three introductions within a few days . . . nothing . . . no reply from Jeffrey.

Later that week, on my regular call with Gerhard Gschwandtner, founder of *Selling Power* magazine and strong champion of my work (who came via introduction from my momentum partner Judy Robinett, remember?), I asked him if he knew Jeffrey. He said yes and immediately introduced us via email. He even asked him to endorse my book within the introduction.

This time Jeffrey responded and agreed to the endorsement.

Then, in the hopes of furthering our relationship, I wrote that I'd love to get to know him better, thank him personally, and see if I could in any way repay the favor of his endorsement. No reply.

I followed up again, this time saying that I'd been listening to his *Sell or Die* podcast, making specific note of one of the episodes I enjoyed. I mentioned that, after reviewing all the past guests, I noticed that he'd never discussed the topic of introverted sales. I mentioned that I'd be honored to help him better cater to that portion of his die-hard fan base. (Notice that the message wasn't about me and why I'd make a great guest but about serving his audience and filling a gap in his programming.)

But still, no response.

Finally, I sent him a LinkedIn message, mentioning that I was heading to Charlotte (where he lived) and it would be a perfect time to do the interview I suggested via email, which I re-forwarded to him, with the dates I'd be in town. Notice, I didn't just send follow-up messages saying, "Did you get my email?" "What did you think of my email?" "Just following up on my email." Instead, each email had new information to consider.

His reply came back: "Yes!"

During our interview, we discussed persistence. He said that he has a "three follow-up" rule. Anyone he doesn't know well, he doesn't typically respond to without a minimum of three follow-ups. He only wants to speak to people who have demonstrated real commitment.

After the interview, he and his fiancée, Jennifer (his podcast cohost and now his wife), mentioned how much they enjoyed the interview themselves and asked if I had plans for the rest of the day. They ended up clearing their entire schedule and showing me around Charlotte. They even did a pretty good job of convincing me that Brittany and I should consider moving there.

A week later, they posted a picture on Instagram, holding my first book, *The Introvert's Edge*, and saying they were "psyched" to read "our friend's" book. What a privilege! And one I would have missed out on if I hadn't persistently followed up.

That's how you tend to your crop of champions. They sometimes require quite a bit of care and attention if you want them to flourish. But these busy people often end up bearing the best fruit.

FOLLOW-UP FOR MOMENTUM PARTNERS

Following up is fairly straightforward for momentum partners.

During your conversation with them, you offered to introduce them to one, two, or three other people. My go-to referrals are usually podcasters, as they are always looking for new and interesting guests, and other momentum partners. I tend not to introduce people to my champions until I've vetted them well, confirming them as givers who have value to offer my prized relationships as well.

Hopefully, your potential momentum partners immediately offered to introduce you to a few of their own contacts as well. Regardless, send your promised introductions at your soonest availability.

If you offered one introduction, send it right away. This shows your potential momentum partner that you're serious about your commitments, and it sets the tone for your relationship. It's all about momentum, which means helping each other and moving quickly. Don't succumb to balance-sheet thinking—remember, you're a giver. Have a little faith that the person is going to reciprocate.

If you offered two introductions, immediately make the first, then wait a few days and make the second. The same rule applies for three introductions: send the first two immediately and hold off on the last.

Why? Because people get busy and forget things. Delaying the final introduction prompts them to think, "Oh, he sent me another and I still haven't sent him one! I better get on that."

Right after sending the first introduction email, send a note via LinkedIn—again, as a personalized invite or message:

[Name], it was a privilege to meet you yesterday, and I really enjoyed our discussion. I just shot you [the introduction or a couple of introductions] I promised you—did you get them okay? You never know with spam filters these days!

I hope they're fruitful.

Speak soon!

For momentum partners, I don't have a timeline for when I expect them to respond. I simply wait to see if they reciprocate. If they don't, that's okay. I know that they're not ready to be a giving momentum partner. It means I got away from a "taker" relationship with only a few introductions. Phew! Plus, I've still given value to a podcast host or one of my momentum partners—so I still came out in front.

FOLLOW-UP FOR PROSPECTS

For prospects, you'll follow up in one of two ways, depending on what happened during your initial conversation.

If they agreed to a follow-up discussion and you scheduled it then and there, your follow-up is simply an email confirming that meeting. Something like this:

[Name], it was great to meet you yesterday, and I'm so pleased you found my guidance helpful.

I greatly look forward to helping you further during our call on Friday the seventeenth at 1:00 p.m. EST.

I'll also follow this email with a calendar invitation.

If you have some spare time between now and then, I'd highly recommend checking out the below post/video/podcast interview: [Link goes here.]

[Briefly explain what it will help them with—this should not be anything promotional in nature.] I think you'll get a ton of value from it.

I look forward to speaking with you soon.

[Follow up with your calendar invitation.]

If you didn't schedule a call at the event, but the person asked you to reach out with some options, then your message should look like this:

Option 1: [Name], it was great to speak with you yesterday, and I'm so pleased you found my guidance helpful.

As promised, below are a few times I'm available to chat further.

[Offer two different days of the week at two different times, one in the morning and the other in the afternoon.]

Would either of these work for you?

I look forward to hearing from you soon.

Option 2: [Name], it was great to speak with you yesterday, and I'm so pleased you found my guidance helpful.

As promised, below is a link to my scheduling app, where you can book in with my calendar directly:

[Scheduling link goes here.]

I look forward to speaking with you soon.

You'll note that in Option 2, I offered a scheduling link. I would highly recommend this, and here's why: an online scheduling tool like Calendly or OnceHub allows you to avoid endless rounds of "I can't do that time—can you do this time?" Not only is this labor intensive, but it also causes prospects to go MIA.

People like instant gratification. When they're ready to book a call with you, they don't want to wait. If they can't lock in with you right then, they'll likely head to Google and look for other options. That's the last thing you want.

Online scheduling software stops this from happening. It gives prospects the peace of mind that they've taken action toward their desired outcome.

With all prospects, just like with champions and momentum partners, you'll also want to send a LinkedIn personalized invitation or message. I'd suggest something like this:

> [Name], it was great to speak with you yesterday. I just sent you an email about [our upcoming/scheduling a] call together. Did you get it okay? You never know with spam filters these days!
>
> I look forward to [speaking with or hearing from] you soon!

From this point forward, just like with champions, you'll want to follow up. You could reach out again with an email (about a week later), then a social message (two or three days afterwards), then a phone call with no message (the following day), and finally a phone call with a voice mail (two or three days later).

It's important to keep in mind that, just like with Jeffrey Gitomer above, you'll want to be following up for a specific reason and with new information to consider. Remember, make your follow-up about them, not you. For example:

> "I'm about to travel to Spain and I know that, when I get back, my schedule will be crazy. So I wanted to make sure

I had you in my calendar, to help you with [briefly speak about the outcome they want] before I left."

"I'm about to go down a hole for a big project and didn't want to disappear without checking in with you. Did you want to schedule that call?"

"I remember you said you have [specific event] coming up, and I know you wanted [outcome] before that. So I thought I better reach out, as my schedule is getting pretty full."

If you still don't get a response, that's okay. After all, *you'd* be teaching *me* if you could land every prospect!

Now, stop for a moment. Sit back and take a breath. With this last piece of the puzzle, you now have all the elements of your networking system—the step-by-step approach that I and so many others have used to catapult ourselves to professional success.

Up until this point, however, it's been all theory, preparation, and practice. In the next chapter, it's finally time to get out of your office and into the room.

the feedback factory

Little by little, a little becomes a lot.

—Tanzanian proverb

Ryan Deiss, the founder of DigitalMarketer, is easily one of the biggest names in online marketing. He's also a huge introvert.

During my interview with Ryan on *The Introvert's Edge* podcast, I said to him, "A lot of people love this new world of digital marketing because they believe it means that they can be at home on their laptop and not really have much contact with people. In this day and age, can you really have a business where you never have to speak to a customer?"

"Absolutely!" he replied. "Eventually."

Ryan then told me a story about the launch of his product DigitalMarketer HQ. He said that, initially, like all products, it was just an idea. But it was one he knew he wanted to create—so he announced it on the stage of his Traffic & Conversion Summit, one of the world's premier digital marketing conferences. He told the audience, "It doesn't exist yet, but if you have questions, or if you're interested in signing up for a beta version, come to the DigitalMarketer booth. I'll personally be back there answering questions."

Over the next three days, he had more than a hundred conversations. "Three of the worst days of my life," as he described them. But, by the end, he knew exactly what people wanted, what they didn't want, what stories worked, and what words triggered emotional responses. Today, he sells a ton of this product on his website, at DigitalMarketer events, and via his inbound sales team—still using all the copy and sales scripts derived from those three days of torture. "We would never have achieved the success we had without those conversations," he said.

What was the real value of those interactions? In a word— validation. Ryan was able to validate, iterate, and refine his message by quickly having conversation after conversation.

That should be your focus too. Now that you have all the elements of a successful networking system, and have practiced your script to deliver it well, the first several times you go out networking should be about obtaining feedback—that's it. The goal is to discover what works, what doesn't, and what inspires interest within your niche.

VALIDATION

When it comes to your initial validation, while of course you want to confirm that your overall script and stories have the desired effect, there is nothing more important than confirming your Unified Message. You need to ensure that it intrigues and excites your niche, not puts them off or leaves you trapped in the same old commodity box.

Jay Kali is a great example of validation at its best.

When I first met Jay, he was really struggling in his online personal training business. While he did have a few regulars, they weren't paying the bills, and he hadn't had a single new client in more than eight months.

As Jay shared his homework within our Rapid Growth® Academy community, it quickly became apparent that, although he'd worked with many types of people, his real passion and a lot of his bigger successes came from helping women regain their strength after pregnancy.

Excited by his new niche, Jay went to work creating his stories and uncovering his Unified Message. With a little support from the group, it wasn't long before Jay had three amazing stories and had decided on a UM: the Strength Architect. All he needed now was a little practice, and he'd be ready to validate it with the world.

He decided to try it out at a conference he'd soon be attending out of town. Of course, you don't need to go to a conference for validation purposes; many of my students just go to a local meetup. And during the COVID-19 lockdown, many conducted their validation through virtual networking opportunities. The conference was a good option for Jay simply because he already had a ticket, and it was the perfect opportunity to test his UM.

After landing at the airport, Jay jumped into a taxicab to head to his hotel. When the driver asked him what he did, he replied, "I'm the Strength Architect." Of course, the driver was curious, so he asked what that was. Jay shared his planned and practiced networking remarks, complete with his powerful story, then ended with his moral, saying, "Does that make sense?"

The driver immediately said, "Yes. In fact, my daughter just had a baby and is looking to get back in shape—do you have a card?"

Later that day, Jay arrived at the conference. During one of the breakouts, attendees were asked to take turns sharing what they did: "I'm a hypnotist." "I'm a copywriter." Person by person, they described themselves in terms of their functional skill.

When it was Jay's turn, he said, "I'm the Strength Architect." This was the only time, out of all the people in the breakout, that someone interrupted to ask, "What exactly is that?" Jay went right into the first part of his networking script and then asked, "Do you know anyone like that?" Many people nodded their heads, and the group leader didn't seem annoyed that he was taking too much time, so Jay continued: "Well, I'm on a mission to help . . ." From there, instead of transitioning into a story, he concluded with, "I don't want to monopolize the group's time, though, so please feel free to find me later if you'd like to chat further."

As soon as the breakout wrapped up, several people asked Jay for his card.

That's a validated UM.

By the way, less than six weeks later, Jay was booked solid.

Now, of course, while I'd love to tell you that validation is always this successful right away, that's not the case.

Remember Nick Jensen, the ex-bull-rider-turned-insurance salesperson from chapter 2? Well, the original UM that he came up with was the Financial Cowboy.

I said, "Nick, while I think it's a cool name, I don't think that's going to get you the desired effect. First, I worry that having the word 'financial' in it is going to lead to people instantly commoditizing you. Second, when I hear it, the first thing that comes to my mind is something risky and dodgy. That's just not you."

But Nick absolutely loved it. He felt that it connected his cowboy past with his new direction of helping small-business owners get to a happy retirement. He really wanted to keep it.

I said, "Nick, it's essential that you feel the name encapsulates who you are as a person, so it's great that you love it. That said, it also needs to resonate with your desired niche. Tell you what—why not take it out networking and see how people respond?"

Unfortunately, as I had worried, the validation didn't go well.

Back to the drawing board.

It wasn't long before Nick had a new name, one I felt perfectly signified his passion for saving the hustlers—the small-business owners like his grandpa—from unhappy retirements. Nick became the Hustle Lifeguard.

Today, as you saw in chapter 2, his new UM makes him much higher sales commissions. And because he's now such a high performer, he can let his family life dictate the hours he works.

Another great example is Charlene Westgate, who you might remember for creating backyard oases that withstand the harsh Arizona heat. Well, originally she wanted to call herself the Oasis Architect. While it certainly had a catchy ring to it, regretfully it failed when it came time for validation. Charlene, while hugely excited about her UM, said that as soon as she shared it with someone, they just fixated on the word *architect*, which put her right back into the landscape architect commodity box.

Like Nick, she had to scrap it. As you can imagine, this was painful for her, as she had written everything out and had practiced, practiced, practiced.

But, trusting the process, back to the drawing board she went.

It wasn't long before Charlene emerged with her new name: the Nature Harmonizer.

And when she took it into the networking room, in her words, "The results started coming in right away." In less than a year, her income exploded, and she'd won two prestigious small-business awards.

While the response to Charlene's and Nick's original UMs might have been tough to hear, getting that feedback—quickly—and then using it to refocus was paramount to their success. Yes, it can be frustrating to have to scrap a UM you love, but it's all part of the process.

This brings me to my last and most important piece of validation advice: you must fully embrace and commit to the new you.

Jimmie Brown is a great example of how easily things can go wrong if you don't.

Jimmie was the owner of a boutique managed service provider (MSP). After talking with him, I could see he helped a lot of businesses with their technology. But where he really shined was helping certified public accountants navigate the complex capacity and security challenges that came with tax season.

If you are not aware, while accountants are open year-round, their workload naturally skyrockets during tax time.

Efficient systems that can handle the extra demand on resources are a must to survive this busy period. The trouble is, many accountants have an "if it ain't broke, don't fix it" mentality . . . that is, until their systems crash in the days leading up to their tax submission deadlines or they get hacked and discover that sensitive client information has been compromised.

I said, "Jimmie, why don't you call yourself the CPA Lifeguard?" I explained that it perfectly signified his ability to help busy CPA firms from drowning under the weight of technology and security challenges.

"I love it," said Jimmie.

"Excellent. Then it's time to go out and validate it."

A few weeks later, after mentioning nothing about a successful validation, Jimmie announced to our online community that his new website was ready and that he was eager to receive feedback.

I reached out to him and said, "Jimmie, while I'm excited to see that you have a new website up, I'm a little concerned. Have you gone out to validate yet?"

"No, not yet. I want everything on my website and LinkedIn profile to be ready first."

I reminded him that validation is not about getting everything ready, it's about getting everything right—*before* putting in any effort creating websites and updating social profiles. It's about ensuring your UM, script, and stories resonate with your niche and get people interested and excited.

Feeling that Jimmie was stuck in a cycle of what I call busy procrastination—doing all the things he could think of except for the one thing he was trying to avoid—I said, "Mate, while what you're doing is great, it's also hiding away. It's time to pick an event, do your research, practice your scripts, and then rip the Band-Aid off and go validate!"

Well, Jimmie partly listened. He attended a local BNI (Business Network International) event.

In the meeting, at the point where everyone gets invited to share a sixty-second pitch about themselves, Jimmie stood up and introduced himself as the CPA Lifeguard, then explained the functional elements of what he did.

One listener, trying to be helpful, said, "What you do sounds like it could really help any business. Can I refer all my business owner contacts to you?"

Jimmie replied excitedly, as if he were about to get hundreds of leads, "Yes, I really can help everyone!"

So Jimmie came back to me and said, "I went to my first networking event and I tried out my UM. But, unfortunately, people saw right through the CPA specialty."

"No problem, it's all part of the process," I replied. "But let me ask you: When you shared your UM, did you get invited to share more, deliver your networking script, and tell one of your stories?"

"No," he said. "I used my UM but there wasn't time for all that." He then walked me through exactly what happened.

"Jimmie, I have good and bad news. The good news is that your UM and networking script didn't fail. The bad news is, unfortunately you still haven't really tested it yet." I explained that after sharing his UM, which took him out of the commodity box, he then spent the rest of the time trying to climb back into it, by reverting to describing his functional skill. This is why it likely all went wrong.

I then brought up my bigger concern. "I'm a little worried about why you said yes to helping any business—and just left it at that. You could have answered that question by saying, 'Yes, I really can help any business owner; however, helping CPA firms navigate the complex capacity and security challenges that come with tax season—that's where I really shine. It's also where my passion lies, which is why I choose to specialize.'"

"I just thought if I agreed, the person would send me more leads."

"That may be true, but every lead you received would just see you as another MSP, who serves anybody, putting you right back into the unmemorable commodity box. With leads like this, price will always be a factor. If you doubled down on your niche, you might get fewer referrals, but they would be perfect for you. They'd see you as the only logical choice and pay you a premium for your specialized knowledge.

"Imagine over the coming weeks or months, a CPA griping about their slow computers or security concerns to any of the BNI members you met. While they might turn down an introduction to 'yet another MSP,' it's far less likely they'd turn down an introduction to a specialist—especially if they recommended you as the CPA Lifeguard."

After I explained all this, I said, "It's time to start again. Pick a totally new event, do your research right, practice your script well, and go validate."

Jimmie's story illustrates the vital importance of not just coming up with a UM and a networking script but truly embracing everything you've put the time into learning throughout this book. Then and only then can you gain the feedback needed to become a master networker.

THE FACTORY LINE

I like to think of my approach to networking like Henry Ford's assembly line. He became famous for the first mass-production automobile; however, his true genius lay in his system of continuous improvement.

If you're a history buff, then you might know that Ford's first production Model T was built in Detroit, Michigan, in August of 1908. The reliable and affordable nature of the world's first mass-production vehicle made it a runaway success. In fact, within days of its release, Ford Motor Company had received orders for fifteen thousand Model Ts.

During the first full month of production, however, only eleven cars rolled off the line. Just eleven. At that rate of production, they would finally have those orders filled in, oh, about 113 years. In an effort to speed up the assembly line, Ford broke it into eighty-four defined areas. Day after day, he tinkered with every aspect of production, increasing the efficiency of each element.

At the end of 1909, less than eighteen months after the first Model T was produced, Ford had manufactured more than ten thousand Model Ts. In 1916, yearly production topped half a million, and by 1927, the fifteen millionth Model T rolled off his Highland Park assembly line.

How did Ford Motor Company increase their production so quickly?

In short, by keeping things simple.

In the early days, Ford's assembly line was kept pretty straightforward. He didn't allow for much, if any, variability. In fact, it was years before Ford started offering his cars in more than one color; you may recall his famous quip: "The customer can have any color they want, so long as it's black."

This is the same focus I want you to have when networking.

Just as Henry Ford prioritized developing an efficient assembly line before adding any bells and whistles, I want you to focus on getting the basics right before worrying about the embellishments.

I want you to become fixated on creating a system that you can control, predict, rely on, and later improve.

After each networking event, do an assessment of how it went. Did they invite you to share more? Did you say your UM and remember to stop? How did they respond? Did you stick to the script? Did it feel conversational? Did you tell your stories well? Did they respond as expected? Were there any curveballs that you didn't know how to react to? For discussions that didn't lead to a call to action, were they in your niche? If so, can you pinpoint where things went off the rails? Is there anything you could have done differently that could have improved the result?

When asking these questions, it's important not to self-criticize.

If you didn't obtain the desired effect, it's not a reflection on you or your personality. It's just an indication that your networking system might need improvement.

Doesn't that take the pressure off?

Trust the system, get a working car off the line—regardless of how wonky it looks or feels—then focus on perfecting the process.

You might accidentally butcher your story or forget to stop talking after you deliver your UM. You may even find that a car doesn't manage to make it through at all, like Charlene's or Nick's UMs. But keep improving the line, keep tinkering and experimenting, and before long, you're going to have a smooth process that consistently and reliably delivers.

If you do this, soon, whenever a new networking opportunity presents itself, you'll be ready for it. In fact, you'll know exactly what to do, and you'll be excited about striking up a conversation—regardless of whether you're at a formal networking function, a corporate event, a conference, or on your next flight. You'll be surprised to discover that the bells and whistles start to come easily too.

Before you know it, you'll have had a series of successful prospect conversations, developed a roster of powerful momentum partners, and have a long list of champions in your corner.

So what are you waiting for?

Let's get your first Model T off the line.

the digital frontier

Nice to be found. Essential to be sought.

—SETH GODIN, seths.blog

I can't imagine what it must have been like for Angela Durrant.

Years of her husband battling cancer had left her stressed out, emotionally drained, and solely responsible for her family's income. While she'd enjoyed many years in her own business as a vocal coach, being the only earner—in a family with a young child and a spouse with medical needs—left her working herself to the bone just to pay the bills.

If that weren't bad enough, within twelve months of her husband's third recurrence of cancer and major surgery, Angela's mother passed away after a long illness. Then Angela herself was diagnosed with diabetes. Her doctor said that she needed to slow down, lose weight, and de-stress—or she'd be the next one in the hospital.

"It was like the last straw," Angela told me. And understandably so—how much can one person take? While they didn't have a lot of money in the bank, she said, "I knew I needed to take a break."

After six months off, however, their savings account was running dry. Luckily, it was about this time that she received a call from Neil Lloyd, the founder of Zokit, a networking and events company in her hometown of Cardiff, Wales. Neil had met her at a networking event a while back and was looking to offer something unique to the attendees at a business expo he was putting on. He asked if she would be interested in running a communication master class in a breakout session.

Angela trusted Neil's faith in her and went to work mapping out what she'd do. She later told me, "It felt a little like divine intervention. It combined everything I knew from my days working for big corporations with what I'd been teaching vocalists for years. I absolutely loved it!" So much so that in January of 2019, she opened up Maverick Communications, to focus on helping managers and leaders better communicate with their teams. She felt that she had finally discovered the business that would turn her life around—a business she loved, with clients who could afford to pay big dollars for the results she knew she could provide.

Unfortunately, as excited as she was about her new venture, after five months in business, she was still earning less than half of her monthly expenses and spiraling deeply into debt.

So Angela sprang into action, applying all the strategies we've been working through in this book, as well as the tactics covered in my first book.

I was thrilled to see that, within days, thanks to her willingness to do the work (and with the help of some very supportive academy members all rooting for her), she decided on her niche (executive leaders), wrote her compelling stories, and created her UM (the Impact Strategist). After a little more preparation and practice, she began going to networking events to validate that everything worked.

Within a month, Angela had locked down a corporate training client and a series of executive one-on-ones, more than doubling her income. Finally, instead of racking up more debt, she was starting to pay it off.

Just sixty days later, she was booked solid. In fact, she even joked, "The validation went too well. I had rapid growth, but I didn't have all the infrastructure in place. So I had to hustle to support it."

Now, I know this sounds like a great problem to have. In reality, however, Angela was just stuck in a new kind of hamster wheel. Yes, she was getting clients; but she had to network constantly to keep bringing in more, all while juggling the demands of a growing business.

Remember, the entire goal of this book is to help you master the room . . . so you never have to go back into one (unless you really want to).

Angela's success, while transformative in her life at that point, was only half the journey. To get off the hamster wheel for good, Angela needed to bring all her success online. This would allow her to tap into a global marketplace, get her ideal clients to seek her out, command even higher prices, and stop the endless hustle for new prospects.

But Angela was resistant to taking this step. No matter how much I prompted her to focus on her online efforts, she held back.

Of course, I understood why. After all, this was the first time in years that Angela could finally relax. She told me, "When I achieved rapid growth and saw all that money coming in, it was such a relief from where I'd been before. I finally had a consistent income—actually, an increasing one. I felt safe."

She went on, "I kept thinking I would get around to all that online stuff. But I was making more than I'd ever made before, and I didn't even have a website up. So I kind of did another month like that and then another. Things were working."

But one morning soon after, tragedy struck yet again when her husband had another health crisis. In the space of just a few minutes, Angela went from a rosy vision of the future to following an ambulance to the hospital. Thankfully, her husband recovered enough to return home. But he was immuno-compromised, which meant that they needed to quarantine themselves—six months before the worldwide COVID-19 lockdown.

Well, now what? Angela's rapid growth had come from her real-world networking efforts and face-to-face coaching, all of which was now virtually impossible for her to do safely.

As you can imagine, without being able to go out and net-work—for fear of bringing even the common cold back to her home—the momentum she had built up quickly came to a screeching and painful halt. Angela now had no choice. If she wanted to continue supporting her family, it was online or bust.

Fortunately, her networking and sales scripts had already put her far ahead of the curve. You see, just as most people have no idea what to say at networking events, they also have no idea how to communicate their value online. But Angela had painstakingly validated, perfected, and proven her entire engagement and sales system. She knew exactly what to say to inspire interest and motivate her ideal niche to buy. All that was left for her to do was to articulate it through digital interactions.

The problem was, Angela was again desperate for quick results, as her income was bottoming out. She didn't feel she had the time to focus on her entire online presence. Instead, she doubled down on just one tactic: LinkedIn.

She updated her LinkedIn profile with her validated and perfected messaging and reached out to twenty people.

Within thirty-six hours, she'd made $3,000 worth of sales, already paid and sitting in her bank account.

Angela shared with our community, "I realize I'm following the model in a slightly backwards way, but this was ground-breaking for me . . . to know that I could make money in one day, even with all the chaos around me."

Shortly after this, an executive approached Angela about working with her one-on-one. When she asked him what drove him to reach out, he replied, "I read your LinkedIn pro-file and it was like you were talking to me. I knew I wanted to hire you before I even got on the phone." He was her first £15,000 client (almost $20,000 US at the time).

What started off as a catastrophe took Angela from provid-ing coaching and training around Cardiff—a population of less than 350,000 people—to serving a global marketplace, charging premium prices, and having clients reach out to her.

As of writing this, almost nine months after getting stuck indoors, Angela still doesn't have a functioning website. All of her online focus is still 100 percent on LinkedIn. Yet she makes more money than she ever did applying my networking sys-tem in real-world conversations. In fact, in April 2020, right after her husband's fourth recurrence of cancer and in the midst of a global COVID-19 quarantine, Angela actually had her best sales month ever.

You never know what life will throw at you. Justin Mc-Cullough went through Hurricane Harvey. Jim Comer's parents suddenly needed his full-time care and attention. Whitney Cole lost three of her long-term customers within a matter of months. My own father was laid off after ten years of dedicated service. And I don't think anyone will ever forget the effects COVID-19 had on millions of offline businesses and "safe" careers.

While of course life would be easier if nothing ever went wrong, the sad fact is, things often do. That's why, even when things are going great—actually, especially then—I highly recommend leveraging your hard work online. It's the last piece of the puzzle to safeguarding your career or business, and it's the key to possibilities far beyond what you could ever expect.

Angela says that if she could tell herself one thing a year before the catastrophic events that befell her, it would be this: "Once you get your networking and sales system validated and perfected, don't get caught up in coasting—even when things look good. Let go of the good to get to the great."

MY OWN FEAR OF GOING ONLINE

I'm almost too embarrassed to admit this, but before I moved to the United States in 2014, I used to think online marketing was a bit of a joke.

Sure, I'd had great business successes, but they were all brick and mortar, leveraging mostly direct sales, telemarketing, and retail stores to acquire new customers. Each business had a website, of course, but it was just enough for people to feel comfortable handing over big checks. Nothing more. That was as far as my online efforts went.

To say I knew nothing about online business would be an understatement. At that time, I was the guy who didn't even know how to change the word *the* to the word *they* on a website. I still remember hassling my then web developers for weeks to make minor changes like this, before eventually getting frustrated and driving to their offices for a two-second update.

When I moved to Austin, however, all that had to change.

While initially my plan was to grow my new business through face-to-face networking, several weeks in, I had a realization: What if I ever wanted to move away from Austin? When I left Melbourne, I left everything behind—my networks, my media contacts, my business partners, and my colleagues . . . everything. By creating a business the same way I had in Australia, I was setting myself up to either be tied to Austin forever or having to start from zero again, should I ever decide to move.

I realized I had to be smarter about how I was building my business—that I needed to give myself the flexibility to take it with me, wherever I went.

I needed an online business, a concept that was not only alien to me but downright terrifying.

Feeling more than a little daunted by the task, I considered just hiring someone to help me. But many of the self-proclaimed "experts" I spoke to clearly struggled to get clients themselves—hardly the people I wanted to trust with my online success. I knew that the only way I could keep my fear and skepticism at bay was to become a student of online marketing myself.

Just as I'd been unrelenting in discovering and creating an effective sales and networking system, I now needed to turn my focus to systemizing the process of predictably attracting new prospects, momentum partners, and even champions online.

I began consuming everything I could on the topic. I listened to three to five books a week via Audible (on 3x speed—we Australians talk fast but we can listen fast too) as well as using text-to-voice technology to listen to at least eight blog posts every day, taking crazy notes the whole time.

Part of my challenge was that there were so many tactics out there. Some just looked like shiny objects, while others promised to be the silver bullet to success. Most of them required months and months of work with no guarantee of results. Even the foundational material was full of jargon and conflicting advice. If you've ever tried to get your head around the world of digital marketing, then you'll know it can quickly start to feel overwhelming.

I also knew there was no way I was going to be on social media all the time, snapping pictures of my lunch or recording impromptu live videos; the whole idea made me anxious. And posting regular blog content, with my reading and writing issues, was also out of the question. This made my search that much harder, as many of the experts were pushing the importance of constantly posting new and fresh content. For me, that would have been a full-time job in itself. No thank you.

But then, after about two months of hitting my head against a wall, it clicked. I started to see the overlap between online and offline sales and marketing, and how it all works together symbiotically. It suddenly became clear that all the hard work I'd done to systemize my networking process gave me a huge advantage online. It was like I had cracked the code.

I could finally see why so much of the advice centered on fancy tactics and huge amounts of hard work. It was because the experts advocating these tactics were trying to help people with bland messaging compete in crowded global marketplaces. They were trying to show you how to win by working harder than everyone else or by employing a "new thing" that no one was doing yet. (But soon everyone was, leaving you with yet another ineffective and time-consuming tactic.)

I discovered there was a way to simplify everything, sidestepping the hustle of online altogether. Not with fancy tools—though I did discover a few that allowed me to automate myself almost completely out of the process—but by leveraging everything that we've already done together in this book. I discovered that, by steering clear of shiny objects and conflicting tactics, I could piece together a basic system that actually worked.

Again, just like Henry Ford, I prioritized an efficient assembly line before adding any bells and whistles.

In fact, I initially didn't even try to make the actual sale online; to me, that was unnecessary complexity I wasn't ready for. I focused instead on using my validated and perfected messaging to get my niche to discover me, be intrigued by what I do, and reach out to me. From there, I took things offline and closed the sale (or fostered a momentum partnership or champion relationship) over the phone.

It worked, and it wasn't even that hard. Just like Angela, I had painstakingly validated, perfected, and proven my entire engagement system. So, even though there's lots of noise in the online world, getting in front of my ideal audience and engaging them with the right messaging seemed to be a breeze.

In fact, after spending just one month and a few hundred dollars setting up my website and social profiles, I didn't tinker with them or touch them at all. I just got too busy.

But that didn't prevent me from attracting high-profile, high-paying prospects directly to my door—almost completely on autopilot and without spending a dollar on advertising (okay, maybe five dollars here and there boosting Facebook posts, but that's it).

It was only in 2017, before the launch of my first book, that I refreshed my website and social profiles to what you see today. And I still leave it all on autopilot instead of worrying about never-ending content creation or the latest social media marketing trend.

Every week I meet people who know a whole lot more than I do about SEO, PPC, or whatever other acronym those jargon-focused digital marketers say is the key to online success. But that hasn't stopped me from making a great income online. In fact, it hasn't even stopped me from getting a bunch of them as clients.

So please, don't get lost in thousands of tactics. Don't overwhelm yourself with multiple shiny objects. Just take what you already have, keep it simple, and build out your first online assembly line. (Check out the bonus materials for a bunch of resources to help get you started.)

YOU HAVE THE ELEMENTS FOR ONLINE SUCCESS

Remember the Strength Architect, Jay Kali, who went to a conference for his initial validation? One of the reasons he chose that route to test his message was that he was an American living in Cancun, Mexico. Validation locally, given the language barrier, would have been challenging.

The language barrier was also a big factor in why he struggled so much to get clients; face-to-face networking and live training wasn't really an option for him. Instead, he offered personal training online, targeting English speakers. But this forced him to compete against both live trainers and the hundreds of other online trainers doing the exact same thing—all with a similar bland message.

But after his successful validation at the conference, Jay simply embedded his message into his online content via Facebook and sent out a few direct messages, like Angela did.

That, with a few basic website changes, led him to being booked solid and hitting a goal he'd set for himself almost five years before—all within less than six weeks from successful validation.

Natasha Vorompiova, the Metrics Whisperer, had a similar challenge. Not because she couldn't speak the language but because her new business was in measurement marketing, an advanced method of analyzing the performance of paid and organic online interactions. Unfortunately, Natasha told me that businesses in her home country of Belgium didn't really engage in a lot of online product launches, which was where she really shined.

After her initial successful validation, she predominantly obtained her growth through interacting with prospects in Facebook groups, sharing her messaging, and providing value. This quickly led to phone calls, where her sales system did the rest of the work. She also focused on giving introductions to potential momentum partners that she met within these groups, who usually repaid the favor.

Today, she has been able to attract several large multimillion-dollar customers and earns a great living doing exactly what she loves.

Then there's Shane, the Arbitrage Architect—who you'll remember as the person who helps doctors leverage commercial real estate in order to get to their happy retirement. After his initial validation, he launched a podcast and was soon approached by the Royal Bank of Canada, as well as a group of three thousand doctors, both looking to partner with him.

And who could forget the story of Whitney Cole, the Mission Maven, from chapter 5? Well, she lived in a remote town outside Milwaukee. Once we identified her niche as health tech companies, networking with potential prospects in real life was next to impossible. So, after her initial validation, she simply embedded her practiced and perfected messaging into a series of online posts via LinkedIn and quickly started getting inbound leads. From there, it wasn't long before her income exploded to $35,000 per month.

The stories of digital success go on and on. However, they could never have happened without the initial work in the networking room.

So, once you've successfully completed your validation and perfected your networking script, it's time to leverage all your hard work into the digital frontier.

And don't worry, I'll be waiting for you in the online resources offered within the bonus materials to help you through the process.

Together, let's amplify your message to a global community.

ACKNOWLEDGMENTS

Brittany, for being an amazing wife and my best friend, for being so patient and supportive while I wrote this book, and for the incredible depth of your love.

Mum, for reviewing my drafts, for all your on-point feedback, and for giving me the confidence to follow my dreams—even when it meant moving to the other side of the world.

Dad, for all your encouragement, for all our late-night talks, for always challenging my thinking, for keeping me focused on what matters most, and for pushing me to be my best.

Chelsea, for always being there to talk and for being the world's best big sister.

Shannon, for pouring your efforts and talents into this book, for putting up with my perfectionist nature, and for being there at crunch time—without you, I'd have been lost.

Derek, for wanting to take this adventure again, for being my trusted confidante, and for our treasured friendship.

Cindy, for being my advocate every step of the way, for your belief in the books I want to share with the world, for being the voice of experience as I navigate the world of publishing, and for being the literary agent every author wishes they had.

Tim, for believing in the potential of the *Introvert's Edge* series and for giving me the time needed to deliver on my vision.

Jeff, Hiram, and Sicily for welcoming me into the Harper-Collins publishing family with open arms.

Jimmie Brown, Whitney Cole, Jim Comer, Angela Durrant, Jon Harris, Leslie Hill, Bethany and Shan Jenkins, Nick Jensen, Jay Kali, Justin McCullough, Shane Melanson, Tarek Morshed, Alex Murphy, Craig and Joel Turner, Natasha Vorompiova, and Charlene Westgate for your willingness to allow me to share your real stories, for your passion for helping other introverts succeed, and your willingness to be vulnerable so that others may learn from your victories and mistakes.

My readers, for trusting me to take you on this journey again.

INDEX

BONUS
Your Exclusive Invitation

---

the introvert's edge inner circle

CONGRATULATIONS!

On completing this book, you have everything you need to transform your networking efforts forever.

Soon, you'll be running circles around the extroverts and feeling a whole lot more comfortable when doing so.

But why stop there?

Let's take your networking game to the next level.

Come join me in The Introvert's Edge Inner Circle—a FREE online community of introverts committed to career and business success.

When you join, you'll receive instant access to a wealth of additional tools, strategies, examples, and exclusive content—including everything you need to dominate in virtual and social networking.

You'll even get to watch video interviews with many of the real people you met in this book.

So, even if you've just started reading . . .

DON'T WAIT.

Access this FREE exclusive content today:

www.theintrovertsedge.com/free-bonuses

Let's start implementing what you've learned, step-by-step.

See you in the Inner Circle!

—Matthew Pollard

ABOUT THE AUTHOR

If you had told me even five years ago that two of my childhood heroes would end up in my rolodex, I would have dismissed you with an introverted shake of the head.

I come from a humble, hardworking family with no "connections." One of my grandfathers was a sheep shearer. The other worked in a factory. One of my grandmothers worked in a cafeteria; the other was a dressmaker. My mother was probably the smartest person in her high school, but when she wanted to earn a degree, her father said: "No child of mine will go to university. You'll go to the best secretarial school in town and learn an honest trade."

So that's what she did. She graduated top of her class and worked as a secretary for many years.

Eventually, though, the boredom of an unchallenging job, plus a growing pain in her shoulders from years of touch typing, got to be too much.

It was around that time that she came upon Michael E. Gerber's book *The E-Myth*—basically the bible for small business systemization—and was inspired to launch her own coaching business. I was only a teenager at the time, but I still remember my parents sitting around the dinner table talking about the issues small businesses faced, how founders get stuck constantly putting out fires, and how systemization is the key to them living happier lives.

Those discussions planted a deep and life-changing seed with me: that most people feel stuck in one kind of problem or another, and that systems are often their only way out.

My mum officially launched her business the following year. However, while passionate and talented, like so many new (and even well-established) business owners, she struggled to find interested prospects. Her saving grace was BNI (Business Networking International, founded by Dr. Ivan Misner). Leveraging the power of what they call "dance cards," she was finally able to secure a group of appreciative, moderately paying, recurring clients.

To me, Michael E. Gerber and Ivan Misner were larger-than-life figures from the other side of the world, who'd given my small-town mother the keys to a better life.

Fast forward almost twenty years. Imagine my absolute shock when a momentum partner of mine offered to introduce me to Ivan Misner. Imagine my surprise when, a few years later, my online networking strategy resulted in Michael E. Gerber connecting with me.

To go from hearing about these titans of small business to having them in my network, not just as contacts but now as friends . . . amazing. Astounding, really.

Like much of my success and good fortune, it happened in large part because I embraced my introversion instead of looking at it as a liability. I harnessed my introverted strengths of preparation, planning, and empathy. I combined these traits with my belief in the power of systems and my commitment to hard work. I networked my way to my dream life and went from talking *about* Michael and Ivan with admiration to actually getting to talk *with* them—and having them in my corner.

Today, I'm on a mission. A mission to help introverts like us realize that we don't have to be (or pretend to be) extroverts. That our path to success is different. When we embrace that, while leveraging the power of systemization, we find our edge, we make our own luck, and we realize our dreams.

It's your turn. Trust in yourself, trust in your abilities, trust in my system—and transform your life.

When you do, reach out and share your success story with me.

I can't wait to hear from you.